WHY I AM NOT A HINDU WOMAN

This book is dedicated to the memory of my parents

Sumati and Chintamani Sonalkar

WHY I AM NOT A HINDU WOMAN

a personal story

Wandana Sonalkar

women UNLIMITED

an associate of kali for women

Why I am not a Hindu Woman
was irst published in India in 2021
by
Women Unlimited
(an associate of Kali for Women)
7/10, First Floor, Sarvapriya Vihar
New Delhi - 110016

www.womenunlimited.in

Reprinted, 2024

ISBN: 978-93-85606-31-1

Cover design: Neelima Rao

Typeset by Manmohan Kumar, Delhi - 110035
and printed at Raj Press, R-3, Inderpuri, New Delhi - 110002

Contents

Acknowledgements

My friend, Anupama Rao, asked if I would be interested in writing a book with this title for Women Unlimited. Once the project was agreed upon between me and the publishers, the long haul began. I thank my family: Ojas, Daryan and Madhura for their support throughout, and for giving me space. My grandson, Riaan, helped me to keep my sense of proportion. I could not have written this without the long conversations I had with Medha Kotwal-Lele, Simrita Gopal Singh, Vasanthi Raman and Ashok Upadhyay. Some of my younger friends in Mumbai listened to bits of my writing and cheered me on: Sangita Thosar, Niranjani Shetty, Sandhya Nare-Pawar, Somnath Waghmare. Telephonic and digital contact with these and many others sustained me through the Covid-19 lockdown which set in as the manuscript entered its final stages.

I am, of course, solely responsible for the book's content.

Introduction

Why I am not a Hindu Woman

This small book has taken me a little more than a year to write, a period marked by tumultuous events relating to my topic. We were well into the fourth year of the first Modi government when I started, by when there had already been significant changes in the political atmosphere, but also acts of resistance, big and small: the assertion by women of reproductive age of their right to enter the Sabarimala temple in Kerala, as well as resistance by Dalit students; by Muslim women; by writers asserting their right to freedom of expression in diverse ways; women asserting their freedom of choice with regard to dress as well as to marriage partner, or even choosing not to marry and to live independently. Across the country were daily assertions, defying an increasingly oppressive Hindu political order and a cruelly divisive social ambience.

Since then, we have had a national election that handed a decisive victory to the ruling Bharatiya Janta Party (BJP), amid misgivings about manipulation of voters through fake news and all forms of disinformation, as well as possibly, about hackable electronic voting machines. We have had state elections, too, in which a central government, only too ready to appropriate all power, has not always found an obedient echo in state assemblies.

So, 2019 saw the ongoing process of establishing a Hindu nation in what we knew and loved as secular India, with all her flaws. My year of writing has taken me on journeys into my past, required me to examine my own beliefs, emotions and convictions and, through the negative assertion that forms the title of this book, given me positive energies to face what the coming years may bring.

At the same time, the rapidly evolving sequence of events as the ruling powers press their agenda of Hindutva into practice has made this book difficult to write, because one seems always to be called upon to react to something new. In fact, there are two distinct registers on which I am holding forth about *Why I am not a Hindu Woman*. The first is, of course, the change that I have referred to in the paragraphs above: the transformation of our secular Indian society into one where Hinduism takes on an increasingly aggressive avatar. This new face of Hinduism is propagated by a government that was voted to power through an electoral process that was once democratic, but has gradually been corrupted: by the manipulation of voters through fake news and demagoguery; the possible selective use of hackable electronic voting machines, a compliant media that sees its role as one of supporting the government rather than raising awkward questions; and, of course, money power, which has always been present, but has now grown to enormous proportions.

This new face of Hinduism may be described as 'political Hinduism' (to echo a term used by Martin Kramer in relation to Islam), the unfolding story of majoritarian Hindu rule, shaped by the ideology that Vinayak Damodar Savarkar called 'Hindutva'. The present regime, like the fascist regimes of the last century, is also supported by and devoted to serving the interests of global corporate capitalism. It is a Hindutva I am, of course, opposed to: I, a woman born into a Hindu family, but an atheist by belief; a feminist; a retired teacher, whose understanding of the world is significantly influenced by Marxism, and who has been trying for decades to understand and oppose the caste system in our society. I am appalled by the increasingly aggressive stance that this Hindutva, or political Hinduism, takes as it insults, vilifies, and declares war on Muslim citizens of this nation. I also understand that this form of Hinduism, while casting Muslim fellow-citizens as the enemy, is essentially a Brahmanical Hinduism. It calls on the Shudras, or middle castes of society, to join ranks in their war against Muslims, while Brahmanical patriarchy, and the caste hierarchy *as a whole*, are kept intact. It is vicious and contemptuous towards women who claim freedom and equality. It makes the miseries, and even the existence, of Dalits and Adivasis invisible, while condoning (and calling for) violence against them whenever they try and assert themselves and claim their rights. It is destructive of the secular institutions built painstakingly after independence which, faulty as they were, still allowed some space for movement, for bringing about change in the highly inegalitarian social order that has prevailed for so long.

I oppose and condemn this political form of Hinduism, which is the ideology of one among many right-wing regimes in the contemporary world, as global capitalism increasingly fails to serve the interests of humanity or of the earth's ecology.

But there is a second register in which I inscribe myself as not being a Hindu woman. This has to do with Hinduism as it is practised in Indian society today, and has been, ever since I can remember. I am not particularly concerned with Hinduism in the ancient past, except inasmuch as its sacred texts, its history and literature, influence the present. Hinduism, as we know it, is inherently misogynist, where most other religions are male-centred. It is based on caste divisions, and one's Hindu identity is always a caste identity. Its casteism and patriarchy are intertwined and can be unbelievably cruel. As a religion, it does not believe in universal ethics or morality, as both are mediated by a range of givens and contingencies. Finally, it places no value on equality.

I am an atheist by belief, but I did not come to atheism through rebellion against the Hinduism I was born into. Rather, through the influence of my atheist father, whose particular brand of non-religious rationalism was, I now realise, in keeping with the spirit of the late 19th-early 20th century Prabodhan or renaissance in Maharashtra. A view that might be described as being close to the Fabian socialists in Britain, together with my mother's gentle non-aggressive religiosity that never questioned his lack of faith, though firmly holding to her own. This meant respect for beliefs different from her own, that was generous rather than pallid, and liberal in a basic sense. Our household was marked by its particular caste: we are CKPs, or Chandraseniya Kayastha Prabhus, a small caste confined to Maharashtra, upper-caste, but not Brahmin, and therefore without a relationship of ownership regarding Hindu religious authority. I say all this because everyday Hinduism is always inflected by caste, though it took me a long time to understand this.

When I moved from this CKP family, living abroad, to a teaching job in a socially backward region of Maharashtra, via an educational moulding in Britain of the 1960s-70s, the reality of caste and its cruelties came to me as a shock. A further realisation of how caste cruelty is intricately linked to the misogyny of everyday Hinduism gradually challenged my understanding of society as I had formed it till then. There was my personal rebellion against restrictions that bound me because of my gender, but because our family was relatively liberal, it was less important. I do not call myself a Hindu woman because caste hierarchy, or Brahmanical power and patriarchy, are integral to Hinduism as it is practised in our society. I will explain and illustrate what this means as I go along.

My Marxism has taught me what I deeply believe: that one understands the world through trying to change it, through practice. I married outside my caste *and* outside my class, and besides the inevitable conflicts within marriage, I have experienced and witnessed what my sons (and my husband) faced because of their caste location.

In late 2018, I felt a strong sense of the moment, the specific juncture in which events of unprecedented historical importance (I hold to this) were unfolding as I set about the task of writing. When I started, we were four years into the first Modi regime, more than 25 years after the demolition of Babri Masjid; 'Project Hindutva' had not only taken off but taken root in society. We had seen the bogey of 'hurt Hindu sentiments' being trotted out in various contexts, resulting in moral policing, mob violence and murder. It had already given rise to the daily harassment of Muslims, with the police turning a blind eye or, at times, actively participating in it. Violence against Dalits was on the increase, and often came down heavily on women. Discrimination against Dalits in educational institutions, or violation of the rules on seats reservation, was being practised routinely and with impunity.

Violence against Dalit and Adivasi women in particular has always been tolerated in villages. Even when a horrific murder like that of Surekha and Priyanka Bhotmange in Khairlanji took place (in 2006), the judiciary and courts responded in a manner that sought to divert responsibility, to cover up the caste motives behind the participation of numerous villagers in the attack.[1] Society and the state have long been complicit in granting impunity to perpetrators of caste violence against women; but lately, the impunity has become widespread, stretching from the vicious trolling on social media of women who express dissident views, including abusive language and threats of gang-rape, to actual killing.[2] It hurt my guts to see that when a young woman of 21, who lost her father in the border war, said that it was war, not Pakistan, that killed her father, she was violently trolled and labelled 'anti-national'.[3] It hurt more because she dared to say the unthinkable.

At whichever point in the past two years that I sat down to write, there were news reports relating to assertions and resistance by women, and consequently, to their being abused and trolled by the Hindu majoritarian regime's sympathisers. In 2018, the Sabarimala temple entry case by women was in the news. The entry of women of reproductive age, between the ages of 10 and 50, into the temple was prohibited by an order of the Kerala High Court in 1991. The Supreme Court, in September 2018, reversed that judgment on the ground that prohibiting women of menstruating age was tantamount to untouchability, and therefore, against the Constitution. Subsequently, women devotees asserting their right to enter the temple were violently prevented from doing so by protesters opposing the Supreme Court judgment.[4]

The prohibition, and the protest by those who support it, are based on two misogynistic principles: first, that menstruating women are 'impure' and 'polluting'; their entry into all temples is prohibited. Second, that the god in the Sabarimala temple is celibate, and the presence of women, presumed to be sexually active, is an affront to his celibacy. But I ask: how can a place of worship be polluted by the entry of devotees going through a natural bodily cycle? How, in relation to the more general prohibitions surrounding Hindu temples, can it be polluted by persons of a certain caste, if they have come to worship the god?

Whereas Hinduism is a faith, a practice, a way of life which includes caste discrimination and patriarchy, but coexists in this country with other faiths, Hindutva is a political ideology that bases itself on hatred of other religions and on reinforcing the caste hierarchy among Hindus. The major context for my declaration that I am not a Hindu woman is the inherent caste patriarchy *within* Hinduism. The instances I have cited, the petition which led to the Supreme Court verdict on Sabarimala in 2018, is just one recent example of it. As a woman born into a Hindu family, I have resisted or questioned the tenets of this religion in various ways throughout my life, even when I did not really understand what I was up against.

So what does it mean, to be or not to be, a Hindu woman?

I have been mulling over this question for some time now, and being, or not being, a Hindu woman is something that brings many aspects of one's existence into play. My body, for a start: in the month of July 2018, when the rains were in full spate, I took myself off to an Ayurvedic resort. There, this widow's torso and limbs were oiled and pounded and steamed and massaged while the rain fell gently on the tiled roof, by young women, two at a time, their fingers practiced and skilful, impersonal enough so that I did not feel any intrusion, just a grateful sensuous pleasure. Only on the fourth day did they bring in a transistor radio and ask me, shyly, if I was troubled by the music. Of course I wasn't: the contemporary songs in Malayalam and Hindi, tunes I usually listen to in my car, were nice to share. By this time I knew a bit about their lives, or at least their work schedules. Ayurveda is not a uniform science all over India: what I experienced here was a series of techniques, medications and diets developed specifically in Kerala.

A Hindu woman's body can become a source of pollution; something that can threaten the efficacy of holy rituals (usually designed to attain very material objectives), pollute a ritually purified space—or even ruin pickles. This happens during menstruation and again, at the actual time of childbirth. But a woman's body can also be dangerous; its seductive power can break the spell of a male ascetic's contemplative exercises. Brahmanical Hinduism places great value on self-control, essentially an attribute, an attainment, of the high-caste *male*: it is he who is capable of voluntary celibacy, bodily discipline, self-sacrifice. For a woman to relate to her own body is essentially destructive. For a young girl to experience puberty in the context of these ideas and practices of exclusion is surely damaging to her sexuality and to her sense of self.

Hinduism allows 'one' to be an atheist, but that 'one' is usually a man. My father was a self-proclaimed atheist, but he did not demur at putting his religion down as 'Hindu'. He saw no contradiction in this; in fact, he rather enjoyed it. But what place is there for a woman who is an atheist? If you're rich enough to be part of a really westernised elite, being an atheist Hindu woman might not be such an anomaly. But I am middle-class. Upper-caste, yes, but middle-class. And although I can say that I've lived my life more or less as I wanted to, the restrictions of, and expectations from, the religion I was born into have made themselves felt at various times and on several occasions. Sometimes through lack of access to spaces I wished to enter, or because of the opinions of those around you that you cannot ignore or dismiss. More often, religion is felt not as a restriction, but as an overwhelming presence, casting a misogynistic shadow over all one's relationships.

Today, I see myself as privileged, economically self-sufficient, and free of pressing responsibility for others. But in the Hindu view I am a widow, a person who has served her life's purpose, and now has no justification for her existence. Of course, modern Hindus are kind to me, refraining from pointing out the superfluousness of my continued existence, saying, 'It is good that you keep yourself busy.' This is one way in which Hinduism daily constitutes the way we see one other, the way we relate to each other. The only way a woman in my situation is accepted is if she embeds herself in a patriarchal family structure, upholding its values and passing them on to the next generation.

I realised long ago that Hinduism is about relationships between people; it lays down norms, and leaves it to us to censure each other if we do not follow them. There is no central authority that frowns on transgressions; there is no single undisputed sacred text that can be referred to. Normativity is always implemented socially. That is how, and why, there is easy legitimacy for those vigilantes we see nowadays, opposing anything from supposed beef-eating to boy-girl friendships or women drinking in pubs. I also think that this is how the caste system has managed to be so durable and so ubiquitous, and also adaptable to change.

This socially exercised normativity is, of course, much more restrictive in rural settings. I was born into a caste that now has hardly any rural roots, and now that I reflect on it, its location has shaped its caste culture to a significant extent. More generally, social normativity is evident in the Indian village through caste patriarchy. Caste shapes the social map of the village, creating single-caste enclaves, and at the same time reproducing caste hierarchy through the relative placement of upper-caste and lower-caste colonies. Patriarchy within the caste, and hierarchy among different castes, both target women, resulting in a social tolerance of violence against them, both on a daily basis and in extreme forms, when there is caste conflict or a violation of the norms of caste endogamy.

This pattern is easily imposed on Muslim, Sikh and Christian minorities within the village. They reproduce themselves in lower-class urban settings, too, with crowded neighbourhoods often being colonised through caste networks, as earlier migrants to the city help out their kin and caste fellows. Many working-class chawls in modern Mumbai, even today, display a more cosmopolitan pattern of settlement, with neighbours belonging to different caste and regional backgrounds. This is true of the Irani chawl in which my late husband spent his childhood and early youth. Of course, these chawls are now being rapidly 'redeveloped' and mill lands converted to sites of luxury towers and malls, with the original inhabitants banished to the outer suburbs of the city. Much has been written about these changes, how caste and class shift and yet reproduce themselves in urban spaces,[5] all of which concerns women very much, as they are required to maintain relationships with neighbours, follow social norms, and (often) impose them on others.

When there was a severe earthquake in Latur district in Maharashtra in 1993(which killed over 20,000 people, completely destroyed 73 villages and affected 700 more) all attempts to break the prevalent caste patterns of housing in the rehabilitation settlements, failed.[6] People just did not want to be resettled in mixed-caste colonies. Residential segregation is very much a characteristic feature of the caste system in India, one which adapts itself to changing situations as 'development' takes place. Even a natural disaster that affects everybody, does not affect everybody in the same way, and does not bridge divides; the tenacity of caste keeps prevalent structures virtually intact.

In the case of the Hindu-Muslim faultline, communal riots can entail a segregation which might not have existed earlier. We witnessed this when we were living in Aurangabad, a city with a significant Muslim minority (30 per cent). After the communal riots of 1988, mixed-religion colonies ceased to exist; we saw our Muslim friends relocating before our eyes.[7] Thirty years on, the Muslim areas are conspicuous for suffering continuous civic neglect. Segregation can facilitate communal tension unless citizens come together to prevent it; but even when riots are prevented, earlier segregation remains.

As a 'Hindu' woman citizen, I am painfully aware of how caste-class hierarchies and religious divides shape living spaces. Moving into modern apartment blocks in Aurangabad and, later, Mumbai, I have been given uninvited assurances by builders that I will not have any Muslim neighbours. Caste is not spoken about so openly, but most middle-class Dalits live in same-caste enclaves. As an upper-caste Hindu woman, I used to be invited to neighbours' all-women gatherings for *haldi-kunku*, where married women, a few weeks after Makar Sankranti, celebrate their 'possession' of a living husband and adorn each others' foreheads with the marks of this status. I gradually opted out, joining only the small-savings groups with my neighbours. Now, in my new home, my widowhood automatically excludes me from the religious ceremony. The much-vaunted 'tolerance' and 'pluralism' of Hinduism applies only to men, whose eccentricities, infidelities, atheism, arrogance and argumentativeness, are ignored by the keepers of Hindu patriarchy, albeit in an approved caste setting. The smallest little girl carries on her fragile shoulders the burden of preserving the honour of her family, her gender, her caste and her tribe.

It is not surprising that those who have, in recent times, found it expedient to declare their position vis à vis Hinduism, have been men. It was in 1995 that Kancha Ilaiah first published his short but fiery book, *Why I am not a Hindu.*[8] He writes as a non-Brahmin, a Bahujan, member of an animal-rearing caste, the Kurumas, in Andhra Pradesh. He argues first, that from childhood, the community he felt himself to be a part of was his caste, rather than some nation-wide religious group. The rituals they followed, the gods they worshipped, and the values that were taught and upheld related to a working life, the devotional practice and morality of an artisanal community. He argues that patriarchy is less toxic when men and women work together.

Ilaiah wrote his book when the first tremors of an aggressive Hindutva tidal wave that has now engulfed us, was rising. It found wide readership, but what is interesting is that, a little more than twenty years later, we have other writers declaring that they *are* Hindu, but that *their* Hinduism is different from the virulent, hate-mongering Hindutva we see around us today. Shashi Tharoor's book, *Why I am a Hindu*,[9] published in 2018, may or may not have been written with this motive, but he argues for the tolerant, syncretic and pluralist aspects of 'Hinduism'. He is widely read, in a literary sense, and quotes selectively from the scriptures and various Hindu philosophers. For example, he cites Vivekananda as saying that Buddhism completed the work of the Vedantic tradition. However, this glosses over the historical fact of the almost complete banishment of Buddhism from India. Caste is presented not as a prescription of the sacred texts, but as practised by the uneducated, rather than by those who read and are acquainted with modern culture. Kancha Ilaiah, in a scathing review, accuses Tharoor of hiding the fact that his own Nair caste is Shudra by status.[10] The matrilineal tradition of the Nairs sanctioned the exploitation of Nair women's sexuality by Namboodiri Brahmins, something that Tharoor neglects to mention. Rahul Gandhi, describing himself as a *janeu*-wearing Brahmin, is perhaps more honest when he tries to project a soft Hindutva, but it is arguable whether he is deliberately asserting his Brahmin status in order to portray the Congress leadership as Brahmanical. The posturing of politicians should not be taken too seriously, and it is doubtful that it is effective in achieving its desired objectives, but it is still an interesting phenomenon *because* they feel the need today to publicly declare their position.

It is not only politicians who feel obliged to go public about their Hinduism. A recent article in Marathi by the well-known stage and film director, Atul Pethe, is entitled *Mi Hindu Ahe*, or 'I am Hindu'.[11] Readers would be well aware that he is not just a Brahmin, but belongs to an elite Chitpavan Brahmin subcaste. He does not mention his caste in the article, but describes how he was brought up to follow certain norms of behaviour, to show consideration to others, and that this was taught to him not just by his parents and grandparents, but also by other families around him. He says, 'The lamp lit before the god at twilight would bring a sanctified peace throughout our home. The persons around me had also taught me that one should not dazzle the eyes of others by pricking them with too intense a light.' I read this as an example of the typical disingenuousness displayed by high-caste individuals in our society. Pethe is aware of, yet does not acknowledge, his superior caste status, his caste privilege. So *his* home (and the homes of his neighbours) become a haven of sanctity through daily religious practise, and in the very next sentence, his sensitivity towards the less fortunate is expressed by avoiding shining too sharp a light in their eyes! Pethe goes on to say that *his* Hinduism is not violent, that he is afraid that those who propagate a violent version of it are endangering his *true* faith. Therefore, he is obliged to defend it.

The above reference is to a text in Marathi. The discourse on religion in regional Indian languages differs significantly from that in English, which difference is, again, more marked in the case of writing by upper-caste individuals. Kancha Ilaiah's book has been widely read in both Telugu and English, but looking for reviews of it I found that no newspaper or journal in English had initially taken the book seriously, either to agree or disagree with him. (Exceptions are Hindutva publications like *The Organiser* and certain blogs.) Later, in 1996, the *Economic & Political Weekly* published a review by Susie Tharu which was largely positive.[12] This, too is interesting: a feminist like Tharu is able to see the pertinence of Ilaiah's text, and acknowledges that she has, over time, been obliged to recognise the relevance of caste for feminism in India. Shashi Tharoor, on the contrary, does not deign to mention Ilaiah's book. Similarly, the largely upper-caste English-speaking liberal Left in India has generally been silent on Hinduism, on the actual daily practise of faith, while being critical of 'fundamentalism' or virulent Hindutva.

To understand this phenomenon it might be useful to look at the argument made by Ruth Vanita in her 2002 book, *Whatever Happened to the Hindu Left?*[13] She poses this question in two main contexts: first, in countries with a Christian or Muslim majority, among persons who claim to be believers, there is both a right and a left wing. Even in India, it is possible to be a Christian or a Muslim with left-wing views: to believe in state intervention to reduce inequality, to criticise capitalism, to support the interests of the poor and the marginalised, the working class. But the Left in India, at least in recent times, finds it necessary to disown Hinduism. Vanita further suggests that this was not the case earlier: the Ramakrishna Mission and the Arya Samaj were reformist associations *within* Hinduism, whose views on many social issues largely converged with communists and the 'secular' Left; but today, the English-speaking liberal Left dissociates itself in the main from Hinduism. As a result (though this is not the point Vanita makes), it is less sharply critical of the caste-ridden daily practise of Hinduism. It simply disassociates itself intellectually, while continuing to follow caste practices at a personal and individual level.

Ashis Nandy, among others, has aptly described the way English-educated Indians were made to feel embarrassed and ashamed of practices such as idol worship which were labelled primitive, backward and barbarous by self-styled modern and enlightened rulers. This did not change after independence. An English-language press coexisted with 'vernacular' media, but, as I said above, the two had disparate frames of discourse. In regional-language media, a Brahmanical hegemony was more overtly present and critiques of caste did not enter the discourse. The English-speaking liberal Left was also largely Brahmin, with a sprinkling of other upper castes, Muslims and Christians. They continued to practise religion in their homes, married largely within their castes, and with Hindu ceremonies, enjoyed Hindu rituals and festivities, but ideologically disowned the polytheistic Hindu faith. This uncomfortable juxtaposition of Hinduism in praxis and atheism or monotheism in ideology meant that the 'secular' Left was completely taken unawares by the rise of Hindutva in the late 1980s, culminating in the demolition of the Babri Masjid on December 6, 1992.

Of course, the central theme of the political project of Hindutva, built up on earlier claims, disputes and legislations, was that the mediaeval mosque known as the Babri Masjid stood on the ground where a Ram temple had existed, at the birthplace of the god in Ayodhya. Culturally, this theme was inculcated into the minds of millions of Hindus through the medium of the *Ramayana* serial broadcast on television in the 1980s. Arvind Rajagopal, in his book, *Politics After Television*,[14] has brilliantly analysed how the airing of this serial coincided with the entry of TV sets into middle-class homes all over the country, as the government pursued a policy of selectively opening up markets for what economists describe as durable consumer goods. Rajagopal also traces the simultaneous spread of a new discourse of Hindutva, or aggressive Hinduism, targetting Muslims through regional-language newspapers, especially in the Hindi-speaking states of north India.

These events paved the way for electoral victories for the BJP, the right-wing party promoting an ideology of Hindutva. Atal Behari Vajpeyi, who was earlier minister for external affairs in the Janata Party government of 1977, served three terms as prime minister of India: 13 days in 1996; then 13 months from 1998 to 1999; and finally, a full term from 1999 to 2004. It was during Vajpeyi's last term in office that a mass killing of Muslims took place at the end of February, 2002, in the state of Gujarat. Its then chief minister, Narendra Modi, was subsequently elected prime minister of India in 2014, with the BJP recording a sweeping victory in parliamentary elections.

Since then we have seen a rise in violence against Muslims and Dalits, with new manifestations of impunity justified by arguments framed by a Hindutva ideology. The stringent implementation of earlier bans on the slaughter of cows, together with some new laws, became the excuse for destroying the livelihoods of Muslims and for lynchings by vigilante mobs of 'cow-protectors'. Sometimes violence is committed against young couples planning inter-faith marriages, or for merely being suspected of doing so. At other times, the murders require no motivation other than the victim being a Muslim. Violence against Dalits, on the other hand, is often a reaction to their assertion of basic rights.

The promotion of hatred for members of marginalised communities often results in the targeting of women and young girls. Hate speech is heavily laced with a venomously misogynistic declaration of patriarchal power. Politicians of the ruling party have publicly applauded perpetrators of gang-rape and murder. It is in such a dangerous and biased atmosphere that we see more and more young women entering higher education and jobs in different fields; these now include a significant number of women from Dalit and Bahujan backgrounds who have to struggle even harder for recognition, but who are also introducing new cultures of resistance in their chosen fields.

I should refer here to two other texts written by men: *Why I am not a Christian*, by Bertrand Russell,[15] written in 1927, and the less-known, *Why I am not a Muslim*, written under the pen-name, Ibn Farraq,[16] interestingly enough, in the same year as Ilaiah, and published in the US in 1995. Russell pares down 'being a Christian' to two essentials:

> When I tell you why I am not a Christian, I have to tell you two different things; first, why I do not believe in God and in immortality; and, second, why I do not think that Christ was the best and wisest of men, although I grant Him a very high degree of moral goodness.

Russell's arguments against the existence of god and immortality are those of a logician and a rationalist. What is more interesting for us here is why he does not believe that Christ was the best and wisest of men (he does not go too far into the question of whether Christ was a historical figure). While he cites several instances of Christ's moral goodness—his advice to give away one's possessions to the poor, or the excellent principle, 'Judge not, lest you be judged'—he points out that very few Christians and Christian institutions follow His example. What Russell really objects to is repeated references to hell and hellfire in Christ's teachings, which have the objective of making people good out of fear. Russell holds that a morality based on fear is unedifying, and here I fully agree with him.

Women have often been considered, by different religions, to be incapable of making moral choices, which has resulted in them being treated with contempt and subjected to violence. I find another line from Russell's text worth quoting here. Having stated the bare minimum of beliefs that define a Christian, he says: 'But for the successful efforts of unbelievers in the past, I could not take so elastic a definition of Christianity as that.' Here, he acknowledges the role of sceptics and non-believers in reforming attitudes to religion. Though he does not explicitly discuss the issue of gender, some of his ethical principles are clearly supportive of feminism. Yet, it is also important for us to discuss gender explicitly.

Ibn Farraq's text is anonymous. It counters the arguments made by some Christians that women under Islam, in its earliest version, are accorded equal status and are respected; that even in marriage both partners enter into a contract as equals. The author vehemently rejects both these claims, even going against some influential Islamic feminists in doing so. He also rejects the practise common among liberal Muslims, of interpreting some of the Qu'ran's pronouncements in a progressive way. I have some scepticism with regard to his arguments, especially when he denies the possibility of progressive interpretations of Islam's sacred texts; there are, after all, various Muslim countries where the official religion is Islam, but whose Constitutions and laws interpret religious prescriptions differently, and in a relatively liberal fashion.

Dr Ramendra,[17] a professor of philosophy, has written on Bertrand Russell, and like Russell, his argument has two strands. The first is a rationalist view that refuses to believe in the truth of the Vedas; being a professor of philosophy, he adds that belief in the authority of the Vedas is common to all schools of Hindu religious thought. Thus, belief in the Vedas, he says, is basic to Hinduism. The second strand is his opposition to the *chaturvarna* system of caste, where he refers to the *Manusmriti* as his source.

Bertrand Russell pointed out:

> In the so-called ages of faith, when men really did believe the Christian religion in all its completeness, there was the Inquisition, with its tortures; there were millions of unfortunate women burnt as witches; and there was every kind of cruelty practised upon all sorts of people in the name of religion.

We are living through a similar age today. The fact that radical Islam may be perpetrating violence across the globe is no excuse for continuing the violence inspired by the politics of Hindutva here, or for continuing to tolerate it. We are witnessing the rise of Christian fundamentalism in Donald Trump's America. We read daily how Zionism, or militant political Judaism, backed by American money and the ideology of war, is committing unspeakable acts against Palestinians: men, women and little children. Even Buddhism, when it becomes a state religion, persecutes and murders religious minorities, as we have seen in Sri Lanka and Myanmar. We have indeed seen enough in recent years of how ordinary people can be instigated to commit horrific cruelties in the name of religion.

Undoubtedly, men who have written on why they reject the extreme violence and misogyny of political Hindutva have some relevance for feminists. And yet, there is a need to go further, to dig deeper into one's personal and political experiences of being female in a Hindu family, of entering the wider world of Indian society as a woman labelled Hindu, and to speak of lessons learned through struggle, both on one's own and in solidarity with others. The shift from Hinduism, whatever that may be, to Hindutva would not have been possible without the profound inequities that are a part of everyday, lived, Hinduism.

Perhaps it is necessary to state here, why I feel I need to do this as a woman. My position within the community of those born into families labelled 'Hindu' is obviously different from someone like Kancha Ilaiah. I belong to a small non-Brahmin upper-caste community with a largely urban presence, and cannot match his claims to the culture of artisanal knowledge. Nevertheless, I feel a statement needs to be made from a *woman's* standpoint, not just from an intellectually or ethically feminist standpoint. The misogyny that is deeply rooted in Hindu patriarchy cuts across castes, and is sustained by caste.[18]

Hinduism has no single religious text. It also has a plurality of ritual practices, local gods and traditional beliefs; yet, in matters of caste and gender, it sacralises inequality among human beings. Writing about why I am not a Hindu woman,

I will have to examine my personal experiences related to issues of caste and gender inequality. This is the moment, the conjuncture, the context in which I, a 60-plus woman, want to elaborate why I am not a Hindu woman. I have had an English-language education and am familiar with metropolitan as well as provincial spaces; I am a feminist, aware of my upper-caste privileges, and willing to take on the challenges posed by feminists of different backgrounds. I have been shaped by my relationships as a child, in my marriage, and now as a mother-in-law, animated by a habit of scepticism and rebellion that has sustained me throughout my life.

References

[1] See Anand Teltumbde, *Khairlanji: A Strange and Bitter Crop* (New Delhi: Navayana), 2008.

[2] For example, the abduction, rape, and murder of an 8-year-old girl, Asifa Bano, in Rasana village near Kathua in Jammu & Kashmir, in January 2018. The victim belonged to the nomad Bakarwal community. She disappeared for a week before her body was discovered by the villagers a kilometer away from the village.

[3] Gurmehar Kaur is currently a student at Oxford University. In 2017, she was violently trolled after she held up a placard saying, 'Pakistan didn't kill my father. War did.' She has since then authored a memoir, *Small Acts of Freedom* which was published in January 2018 by Penguin Random House.

[4] See, for example, report in theWire.in, October 16, 2018.

[5] See Neera Adarkar and Meena Menon, *One Hundred Years One Hundred Voices: the Millworkers of Girangaon: an Oral History* (Calcutta: Seagull Books), 2004. See also 'Caste and Gender in a

Mumbai Resettlement Site,' by Varsha Ayyar, *Economic & Political Weekly*, May 4, 2013.

[6] S. Parasuraman, et al, *Organisation and Administration of Relief and Rehabilitation Following Marathwada Earthquake, 1993* (Mumbai: Centre for Research on the Epidemiology of Disasters, Tata Institute of Social Sciences, Bombay), 1995, p. 322.

[7] See Asghar Ali Engineer, 'Aurangabad Riots: Part of Shiv Sena's Political Strategy', *Economic & Political Weekly*, June 11, 1988.

[8] Kancha Ilaiah (Shepherd), *Why I am not a Hindu: A Sudra Critique of Hindutva* (Kolkata & Delhi: Sage Samya), 2018.

[9] Shashi Tharoor, *Why I am a Hindu* (New Delhi: Aleph), 2018.

[10] See Kancha Ilaiah's review of Tharoor's book: 'Swami Shashi: The Political Hinduism of Shashi Tharoor', *The Caravan*, May 1, 2018.

[11] Atul Pethe, '*Mi Hindu Ahe*', *Loksatta Sunday Edition*, September 9, 2018.

[12] Susie Tharu, 'A Critique of Hindutva-Brahminism', *Economic & Political Weekly*, Vol. 31, No. 30, 1996.

[13] Ruth Vanita, *Whatever Happened to the Hindu Left?* New Delhi: *Seminar*, 2002.

[14] Arvind Rajagopal, *Politics After Television* (Cambridge: Cambridge University Press), 2001.

[15] Bertrand Russell, *Why I am not a Christian and other Essays on Religion and Related Subjects* (UK: Touchstone), 1927.

[16] Ibn Farraq, *Why I am not a Muslim* (New York: Prometheus Books), 1995.

[17] Ramendra Nath, *Why I am not a Hindu*, Bihar Rationalist Society (Bihar Buddhiwadi Samaj), 1993.

[18] The resistance to caste patriarchy within Hinduism has been asserted by women of all castes and by shudra-atishudras (to use the terminology of Jotirao Phule) of all genders across centuries. See Jotirao Phule, *Selected Writings of Jotirao Phule* (trans. G.P. Deshpande, New Delhi: Leftword Books), 2002.

1 The Hindu Family

Men who oppose their own religion usually rely on rationalism and some sort of public ethics to bolster their arguments, and are usually unaware of the gender aspect. But in writing *Why I am not a Hindu Woman,* I find that this is not enough. I understand Hinduism to be a system of caste patriarchy, which has also been described as Brahmanical patriarchy. A central institution of this caste patriarchy is the family. While most religions have a patriarchal family structure at their core, my personal rejection of Hinduism must start from the Hindu family as I have experienced it, at various stages in my life. This repudiation is thus, necessarily more personal than men's rejection of religion on the grounds of rationalism and generalised ethical values.

A Hindu woman's relationship with religion is, first and foremost, tied up with the home, housekeeping, and the hearth. Swami Vivekananda, despite a somewhat rationalist approach to Hinduism, was not free of the caste and patriarchal values that it embodies, and he was not addressing only women when he said,

> There is a danger of our religion getting into the kitchen. We are neither Vedantists, most of us now, nor Pauranics, nor Tantrics. We are just 'Don't-touchists'. Our religion is in the kitchen. Our God is the cooking-pot, and our religion is, 'Don't touch me, I am holy'.[1]

My rejection of Hinduism is that of an upper-caste woman who experienced caste-based humiliation relatively late in life, and in a relatively mild form, after I married outside my caste. My declaration, therefore, that I am not a Hindu woman is based on a more complex reality, and on my gradually evolving understanding of this reality.

Tolstoy famously began his great novel, *Anna Karenina*, with the words, 'All happy families are alike; every unhappy family is unhappy in its own way.' Mine was an overtly unhappy and dysfunctional family, and so it could not, even at a stretch, be seen as an advertisement for Hindu family values. The happy family, nested within the moral boundaries and the social and sexual regulations of patriarchal hetero-normative religiosity, is what shapes the ideal Hindu individual. Happy families are a construct; unhappy families have stories. It is perhaps because I grew up in an unhappy family that I never really believed in the imaginary ideal of the Hindu family as an institution; but it *is* an imagined ideal, and trying to live up to it often adds unnecessary strains and stresses to the normal tribulations of family life.

The construct of the happy Hindu family pervades our religious texts, and certain kinds of literature. First of all, the *Manusmriti*. Of course, it lays down the (in)famous rules for the duties of women thus:

The duties of women

147. By a girl, by a young woman, or even by an aged one, nothing must be done independently, even in her own house.

> 148. In childhood a female must be subject to her father, in youth to her husband, when her lord is dead to her sons; a woman must never be independent.

But, before that, we have:

> 55. Women must be honoured and adorned by their fathers, brothers, husbands, and brothers-in-law, who desire their own welfare.
>
> 56. Where women are honoured, there the gods are pleased; but where they are not honoured, no sacred rite yields rewards.

These rules and the accompanying advice are addressed to the male householder. In fact, the *Manusmriti* is addressed to the *upper-caste male householder*, laying down laws of morality and the prudent treatment of one's inferiors (women, Shudras and Atishudras, or Dalits). Women are not expected to act independently, so their only morality is to obey the men of the family.

> 154. Though destitute of virtue, or seeking pleasure elsewhere, or devoid of good qualities, yet a husband must be constantly worshipped as a god by a faithful wife.
>
> 155. No sacrifice, no vow, no fast must be performed by women apart from their husbands; if a wife obeys her husband, she will for that reason alone be exalted in heaven.

Yet, having deprived women of any will or conscience, even the *Manusmriti* finds them to be mysterious creatures, possibly endowed with magical powers:

> 58. The houses on which female relations, not being duly honoured, pronounce a curse, perish completely, as if destroyed by magic.
>
> 59. Hence men who seek their own welfare, should always honour women on holidays and festivals with gifts of ornaments, clothes, and dainty food.[2]

How to appease these mysterious beings who hold the well-being of their families in their hands, is also explained: by giving them gifts on auspicious occasions.

The influence of the *Manusmriti* can be seen in attitudes towards women in Hindu society. The Puranas contain many examples of tales that portray women as fickle, sexually rapacious, and untrustworthy. On the other hand, there are many examples in modern (20th century) literature in which the ideal Hindu family is portrayed typically as a Brahmin family, where the mother makes all kinds of sacrifices for the sake of her children—in the main, her sons—and teaches them the desired values that should guide them in life. In Marathi literature, a famous example of this is the novel, *Shyamchi Aai* (Shyam's Mother)[3] by Sane Guruji; it is the story of a boy growing up in a Brahmin household in a rural setting, with special care bestowed on him by his mother who inculcates in him the value of kindness, above all. The novel was a childhood reading staple for schoolgoing boys and girls of my generation in Maharashtra, and was made into a popular tear-jerker, a five-handkerchief movie, in 1953. Shyam's family, with all the features of a Brahmin household, became a kind of role model for *all* castes. TV serials usually depict the same family model, but with something going wrong, maybe through the machinations of a wayward woman, but brought back to the true path by a virtuous woman who forgives errant men, observes the rituals and calls down the blessings of the relevant god. Even serials that have a 'progressive' theme related to women are inevitably placed in a Brahmin setting.

Part 1: A Hindu family in Singapore

My family left India for Singapore in 1953, when I was barely one year old. My father was appointed manager of the Singapore branch of an Indian bank, where he stayed for the next twelve years. I am the youngest of four children. My eldest brother and sister were left behind in India with my paternal grandmother, as they were finishing school and entering college. My brother Sudhir, nine years older than me, started going to school in Singapore, then still under British rule.

We lived in a spacious bungalow that became the unchanging location of my earliest memories until I was 11. Our home help, Sikh and Malay, were assimilated into a 'greater Indian' community by my parents on an island where Muslims and Sikhs had their place. My mother was used to having servants to help her with cooking and other household chores, though she was a good cook herself. In Singapore we had Malay servants; back in India they would have been from the lower castes, though not Dalit as a rule, although my mother, claiming that she did not practise untouchability, would point to how they had had a Dalit house-help when they were living in such-and-such a place.

In India, too, though my father's job took him to cities all over—pre-Partition Karachi and Dhaka, among others—their social circle was confined to their own caste and Brahmins. In Singapore, their social circle was cosmopolitan, and they had an active social life. Singapore then, had a large Indian population; third in number after the majority ethnic Chinese, who were about 80 per cent, followed by indigenous Malays, about 15 per cent. Most of those of Indian origin were Tamils, descendants of indentured labourers. Then there were Sindhis, Gujaratis and Punjabis in business, making the most of this commercial city and entrepôt port. When black-and-white television arrived in Singapore, much was made of the fact that broadcast time was divided among four languages: English, Chinese, Malay, and Tamil.

My mother often spoke of how she became more involved in Hindu religious ritual after her first pregnancy. She had fallen ill and had to be cared for by her mother-in-law, my paternal grandmother. In gratitude, and from a sense of obligation, she gave in to all that was demanded of her, and was thus initiated into the world of lengthy puja rites, complicated practices of ritual purity, particularly on fasting days, and even a familiar set of superstitions.

These confidences about her early married life and the reasons for her taking up so many devotional practices, usually followed the frequent clashes she had with my father over these religious observances. He was a self-proclaimed atheist, but with a fairly comprehensive knowledge of the Hindu shastras, and his loudly chanted Sanskrit shlokas are an indelible part of my childhood memories. One such memory is of his satirical chant in Marathi: 'O God, my God, what is to become of you?' rather than, 'What is to become of me?' He would then berate my mother for spending long hours in front of 'her' gods, reading aloud from the Puranas. 'Are you even aware of what you are reading?' he would ask, 'those stories are full of prostitution, thieving and debauchery.'

Our house in Singapore provided my mother with an especially congenial setting for her religious worship—a separate puja room, a luxury she had never enjoyed before. There was space there for all her framed pictures of gods and her murtis. I remember, particularly, the picture of Datta accompanied by his dog, and one of Sai Baba; the crawling infant Krishna and Hanuman also remain in my memory. There was an image of the goddess Saraswati, and on the wall a large framed Ravi Varma print, depicting the sage Vishwamitra repudiating the apsara, Menaka, who has broken his meditation. There were niches in that tiled room for her holy cloths, squares of unbleached silk, stained yellow with turmeric, sacred and not to be touched by us, unreliable children that we were. My brother Sudhir would later say of her, with a hint of pride mixed with exasperation: 'My mother is the only woman in India who believes in untouchability, but doesn't believe in caste.' This was because she often treated us children as 'untouchable' on certain days when she did her pujas or observed fasts that required a high degree of ritual purity. She had separate vessels for cooking her food on these days, and separate stores of tea and sugar. We were not allowed to enter the kitchen once she had swabbed it herself before cooking her special fasting-day meals, though of course we were allowed to partake of the delicious saboodana khichdi or the other dishes once the gods had blessed them.

It was later, when we were living in India, that my brother repeatedly made his claim about my mother's purity-pollution practises. She did treat us children as untouchable, as unreliable sources of pollution, because we were not willing to follow her rules and she chose not to impose them on us. This was not for fear of my father's wrath: I think there was a genuine spirit of liberalism in our family, which she too respected, though she chose to follow a more traditional path herself. But as relations between her and my father worsened and our family became more dysfunctional, that white-tiled puja room and its less commodious successors became a refuge for her, an oasis of peace and selfhood. This is common to many Hindu women, especially of the upper-castes, who have access to a designated sacred space within the home. The pollution rules were a means of defending that territory, but they were also an attempt to emulate Brahmins.

I grew up looking at my mother's ideas of purity and pollution as absurd, but no more than a somewhat lovable idiosyncracy, a sentiment that found expression in my brother's words. I was not so sure about the second part of Sudhir's declaration, however, that she didn't believe in caste—she was always conscious of being upper-caste and upper-class, always expected to have servants on hand, whom she could depend on for diverse services. She was the only girl from her family who had been to college; in those days her college classmates and friends would have been Brahmin women. I know that the few friends she spoke about and met up with after her return to India were Brahmins, and she perhaps had something of the 'CKPs are almost Brahmins' attitude that is sported by some members of this caste. She was definitely displeased that I chose to marry outside our caste, and that my husband belonged to one she considered to be lower in the caste hierarchy.

The *Manusmriti*'s first mention of women is that they should have a place of respect within the home; that a home where the woman is happy is a place of sanctity. This is an idealisation of the Hindu home, a description of how idyllic it can be *if everyone plays their part.* Caste patriarchy lays out an assigned role for everyone; glorifying the woman's role is tantamount to glorifying the family as an institution. It is only later chapters of that text that spell out how subordinate that assigned role is, even for the high-caste woman: she is not free to take any decisions on her own; and is equated to the Shudra whose only duty is to serve others. The Brahmin, the twice-born (male) householder, is enjoined to keep her happy with ornaments and gifts. This picture of a serene Hindu home with the sacred puja corner bedecked with flowers (which, even when dry, can never become garbage; they are *nirmaalya*, or that which cannot be polluted) and the air heavy with the scent of joss-sticks, has definite caste overtones in the *Manusmriti*. It is an image repeated endlessly on our television and movie screens, and the setting is always a well-to-do, upper-class home.

Of course, these and related images have an alluring aspect, too. Lighting a lamp at dusk, also usually the woman's duty, has heavy emotional overtones in Marathi literature and culture. There is a link with the past when a lamp lit outside the (rural) home served a practical purpose, as well as the magical/ superstitious/ primeval one of warding off evil spirits. In today's urban homes, the lamp is lit inside the house, before an array of images of household gods. The woman's hand lighting the lamp, or the mother's voice reminding her children to do so, becomes a powerful symbol of the role of the Hindu woman in keeping the home safe, happy and protected. In Maharashtrian homes, there is a recitation that takes place at this time: the Shubham Karoti. It starts off invoking all things auspicious for the home, the welfare and good health for all its inmates, and of course, wealth. And then the line where the recitation ends:

Diva laavlatulshipashi,
Ujedpadla Vishnpashi

The lamp is lit by the holy basil (usually in a *tulsi-vrundavan* in the garden outside) representing the goddess Tulshi, but illuminates the place of Vishnu, who is Tulshi's husband. The woman's hand lighting the lamp at twilight illuminates not the female deity Tulsi, but the male god, Vishnu. All devotional acts are carried out so that the male householder remains protected, safe and well, and the patriarchal order remains intact. A friend whom I consulted on this, a feminist from a Brahmin family, says it gets worse in later verses, which actually ask for the *dhani*, the male householder, to remain alive and well, this being equivalent to the well-being of the entire household.

It was while my grandmother was staying with us in Singapore that we regularly gathered in the puja room to sing aartis in the evening. My father did not oppose this. In the month of Shrawan (which falls during the monsoons in India, but had no connection with the seasons in equatorial Singapore) there were several festival days on which specific kinds of sweets were offered to the gods, and then to us. Since the house was big and the large kitchen was at one end, I don't remember how my mother managed these occasions with her Muslim help, Esah; my mother's cooking was traditional, Maharashtrian and specific to our CKP caste.

We sometimes visited the Ramakrishna Mission in Singapore, which gave me a glimpse of a Hindu religious institution. I think the purpose of our visits was for my father to make charitable donations, while he acquainted us with a more 'rational' version of Hinduism. He was not very articulate on such subjects, but I found the place had an atmosphere of peace. I now learn that the Mission was established in Singapore in 1928, and that the Boys' Home was a result of its sheltering orphaned male children during the Second World War.[4]

On February 26, 1960, an Alitalia flight headed from Rome to New York took off from Shannon Airport in Ireland, after refuelling. It had hardly gained height when it crashed into a nearby graveyard, went up in flames and killed 34 of the 52 passengers on board. One of them was Mr S, a film distributor based in Singapore, who left behind a widow and two sons. This family belonged to our close social circle. That air crash was the beginning of a tsunami that engulfed our family and turned it upside down. By lending Mrs S a helping hand, my father began an affair with her that lasted till the end of his life.

Part 2: An unhappy Hindu family

I must make a declaration here: I realise that in this chapter I am writing about why *I* am not a Hindu; I, an upper-caste woman who did not suffer directly either from caste or patriarchy in her childhood, but my emotional traumas were a consequence of the patriarchal context in which my parents' marriage fell apart. The caste background of some of these circumstances only became apparent to me later. My rejection of Hinduism was not a black-and-white process, but there is a political purpose in my writing about these early influences. We expect autobiographical writing about caste to come from Dalits, for whom the humiliation and suffering are the greatest. Upper-caste writing is usually less frank; the 'proud-to-be-a-Brahmin' ethos hovers over much of it, and usually results in blindness to one's own privileges. Upper-caste feminist writers will dwell upon the outrages men commit, and on the inequity of patriarchal family structures, but less on the ambiguities of women's responses. My account of my dysfunctional patriarchal family is intended to be neither a condemnation, nor a defence. I prefer to invite my readers to reflect on how, with its variations and its ability to change, Hindu patriarchy is founded on inequality and worse: on regarding certain bodily functions, certain socially necessary tasks, and certain fellow human beings, as impure and polluting.

My father was the eldest child of my grandfather's second wife; his first wife had died after bearing him three sons. My grandmother was married at the age of sixteen, unusually late for those times. In all, she bore four sons (one of whom died at the age of six after my father was married) and three daughters. My father was elder brother to six siblings, all of whom adored him, but the real patriarch was my grandfather's eldest son, whom we called Dadakaka, a tall, stern and forbidding figure, whom my father looked up to. Dadakaka had made his career in banking, and my father, after trying out other jobs, followed him, joining the Central Bank of

India in 1934. He met my mother at several family weddings; the two fell in love and married in May 1935.

My father was a science graduate, having studied at colleges in Bombay and Karachi, and had seriously considered doing research in physics before he took up a job in the government. My mother was an arts graduate from Morris College in Nagpur, and used to say that she would have preferred it if my father had chosen an academic career. My mother was the only one among six sisters to have gained a college degree (in 1935).

My father was a benevolent patriarch for the younger members of the family, one who believed in women being educated even through college level, which was not so common those days. My mother supported him, and they were a well-matched couple in many people's eyes. Their marriage was the catalyst for at least three couples among our close relatives to also have 'love marriages', two of which reinforced the marital bond between my mother's family and my father's.

My father was outgoing, generous, with great personal charm. He wanted to be liked and he was. My mother was quieter, quite content to live in his shadow, and to be appreciated for her cooking and her ikebana flower arrangements, which became a favourite pastime. When my brother Sudhir began writing poetry and showed it to the writer, Prabhakar Padhye, he remarked, 'You have inherited your mother's gentle gifts.' Sometime later, after the family had been jolted by my father's affair, she even translated a novel by the Japanese writer, Junichiro Tanazaki, into

Marathi, from the English, a novel about an extramarital affair. The suggestion that she translate it came from Marathi author, Shri Na Pendse, whose brooding, incestuous novels were set in the Konkan region.

My father's combination of liberalism, in conduct and in values, together with an excess of generosity and a lack of snobbery, could be associated with our class, but I now realise that his generosity came from being a member of a small caste that was economically and educationally privileged, but did not have the same power in the hierarchical caste order, the same sense of entitlement, as Brahmins. It may also have had something to do with his being his mother's eldest son, responsible for the welfare of his younger brothers and sisters. 'Liberal' in his case included his atheism, his enthusiastic support for women's education, his benevolent patriarchy, and his lack of discrimination between his sons and daughters.

Besides their busy business-related social life, my parents had few friends in Singapore. The two families we interacted with most were a childless couple from Assam, among the most intellectual people I came across in my childhood; the second, a Sikh family, where the husband worked in the Indian embassy and his wife sometimes played golf with my father. The third was the family of Mr S, Saraswat Brahmins from Mangalore. When he died in the Alitalia air crash of 1960, my father extended his usual helping hand to Mrs S, whom we knew as Aunty M. She was entitled to a hefty insurance payout, but obtaining this required considerable time and effort with lawyers and accountants. The S's lived in a flat not far from our home, but soon after the accident Aunty M moved in with us. There was nothing unusual in this for our family; but my father's helping hand soon led to a tempestuous affair between them. My mother tolerated Mrs S's presence for a while, but then insisted that she go back to her own home. She did, but the affair continued. My mother was left with no one to confide in, no one who could support or guide her. I was a somewhat precocious child and was aware of what was going on, but, of course, could not talk to anyone about it.

What I found most disturbing about this situation, besides my mother's pain, was the shroud of dishonesty that descended on all our interactions. Nobody talked about the elephant in the room. Sometimes the servants taunted me about it. The Pacific Ocean tsunami of 1960 that was all over the newspapers later that year echoed my feeling of upheaval and haunted my recurrent nightmares for a long time. So here was a Hindu family in crisis, and the cracks showed up all the caste-and-patriarchy-based contradictions in its structure. We grew up with a set of liberal values, a fair amount of gender equality, and we certainly expected that a love marriage like my parents' would be monogamous. But the spirit of Manu hovered over us, making my father's affair acceptable to many around us, even if not to be talked about openly. After all, Manu says:[5]

> 12. For the first marriage of twice-born men, wives of equal caste are recommended; but for those who, through desire, proceed

> to marry again, the following females, chosen according to the direct order of the castes, are most approved.
>
> 13. It is declared that a Shudra woman alone can be the wife of a Shudra; she and one of his own caste the wives of a Vaisya; those two and one of his own caste the wives of a Kshatriya; those three and one of his own caste the wives of a Brahmin.

The CKPs, like many economically well-placed non-Brahmin castes, claim to be Kshatriyas but have an uneasy relationship with Brahmins. They are not authorised to perform religious rituals, for example, they need to call on a Brahmin for this. This difference in status in the caste hierarchy makes for an almost intangible difference in their sense of entitlement. Others, even slightly lower on the caste pyramid, never have the same sense of ownership of the status quo. The ideal Hindu family, then, advertising Hindu ideals and values to the world is, by definition, the Brahmin family.

I now feel that there may have been a caste aspect to how this extra-marital relationship played out in our family. Mrs S was a Saraswat, a Brahmin subcaste originally located in the coastal regions of Maharashtra and north-west Karnataka, that spoke Konkani, and whose food habits were not very different from ours. She entered our home with complete confidence, first in Singapore and later in London, and complained to my mother that her children (that is, we) didn't treat their Aunty 'nicely'. (It was mainly Sudhir and me whom she came into contact with, and although we were never openly rude we did not hide our resentment.) The *Manusmriti* lays down caste-based rules for a man who wants more than one wife; it would be a *pratiloma* relationship, one that went against the grain. My father had the patriarchal upper hand; divorcing my mother was never on the cards.

My mother withdrew into even more lengthy puja rituals and more frequent fasts, eliciting outbursts of contemptuous anger from my father, but her religion seemed to be more and more inadequate in terms of guidance or succour. She did not believe in godmen, gurus, or similar soothsayers, in contrast to Mrs S, who was a devotee of Satya Sai Baba. With his overflowing curly hair and decidedly this-worldly countenance he was a striking contrast to the original Sai Baba, whose picture had pride of place in my mother's puja room. My mother's Sai Baba, as even I was aware, was revered by Hindus and Muslims alike. Mrs S also offered novenas at a local church, for special favours. I was perplexed by the fact that what I saw as a more genuine form of devotion in my mother brought her no comfort or relief from pain. Seeing her in this distress reinforced my later rejection of religion as I grew up.

The extended Hindu family offered neither solace nor support. When we made one of our three-yearly trips to India later that year, the elephant in the room was never mentioned. My father enjoyed the same respect and affection as always, and when we returned to Singapore things went back to being just the same as before: a family that kept up appearances on the outside. Much later, some of my older female cousins expressed their indignation against my father and sympathised with my mother, but my grandmother objected: 'Don't anybody say anything to my son, he is very sensitive.'

Both the extended Hindu family and its nuclear version in the diaspora are highly patriarchal institutions. True, it was only in 1955—not very long before these events—that India passed the Hindu Marriage Act, a law forbidding polygamy in marriages registered under it, and allowing women to initiate divorce on specified grounds. Ambedkar had resigned as law minister in 1951, after Parliament rejected his Hindu Code Bill which codified these and other principles of caste and gender equality, as it was vehemently opposed by traditional Hindu members.[6] Polygamy, or at least, bigamy was, and is, practised among Hindus at least as frequently, proportionately, as among Muslims. The orthodox Hindu (mostly Brahmin, and male) objectors did not appreciate that Hindu men could have only one wife, while Muslims, under their personal law, were allowed four. Women having the right to initiate divorce would break up the Hindu family as an institution! I wonder whether these debates in Parliament had been discussed within our extended family; certainly my father was looked upon with indulgence, and not a little envy, by his generation of male members. My generation, including my older cousins, on the other hand, seemed to have absorbed the idea that marriages in modern India should be monogamous, so several, on my father's as well as my mother's side, sympathised with my mother. In any case, after twenty-five years of marriage, with two adult children who were not yet economically independent and two younger ones, with no means of earning an income herself, my mother could not on her own contemplate divorce. Moreover, there was nobody who would take the initiative to even suggest the idea to her.

When the patriarch is the lynchpin that holds the family together, how does a Hindu family cope when he himself strays? The first reaction is to brush everything under the carpet, to pretend that nothing is amiss. Silence around sexual matters is one characteristic of modern Hindu society that has devastating consequences for the sexuality of both men and women. The framework of patriarchy and of caste, both allowed for Mrs S's presence in our house and brought with it the need for secrecy and hypocrisy. My father did show some signs of being wary of the social disapproval of his defiant relationship with Mrs S: he shied away from negotiations when my eldest brother's marriage was being arranged, and was relieved that his younger children did not contemplate arranged marriages.

During this period, visits from a few prominent figures in Marathi literature provided some relief for my mother. Mrs S somehow became invisible at these times; I can imagine that this would have been humiliating for her. My father, of course, enjoyed the best of both 'worlds', and as long as we were in Singapore, away from close relatives, he was shielded from social disapproval.

My own relationship with my father was complicated. He adored me, his youngest child, and tried to compensate for his guilt by becoming over-protective. For me, he was always a flawed father figure, but a loving one. That love gave me a sense of self-worth which has shielded me throughout my life. At the same time, it was painful to see my mother's suffering. I tried, in my imagination and in my own childish way, to reconcile the two of them. I couldn't, naturally, and that induced an overwhelming sense of failure. This sense of failure stayed with me well into my adolescence, and maybe through life.

My portrayal of a Hindu family in crisis is not written from an experience of great personal suffering, rather from my sympathy for my mother even though, as a child, I was closer to my father. These conflicting pulls and confusion of emotions awakened in me an incipient sense of injustice. There was a clash between the liberal values we had been taught and which I absorbed, and my father's behaviour. At the same time, I also rejected my mother's passive acceptance of the situation. Our family became more dysfunctional as time went on, and especially after my parents returned to India. My father bought a flat in Pune, but lived in Bombay himself with Mrs S, in Mahim. My mother, living without her husband in Pune, was looked upon with a sympathy that made me cringe. My brother's and sister's lives were a mess. Sudhir sank into psychological depression and a drinking problem. My sister, Kalpana, practising as a doctor in a poor area of Pune, was never able to make ends meet and slipped into poverty. I moved away from Pune, taking socially risky decisions that were prompted by a desire to escape from the family situation. And yet I could never get away, even after

I married; the ties binding me to this dysfunctional family were like strong elastic bands.

Much later, I became aware of another impact that my father's affair had on my self-image, when I read a book called *Akkarmashi*,[7] by the Dalit writer, Sharankumar Limbale. *Akkarmashi* is a term used to describe gold that is adulterated. Limbale is the son of a Dalit woman who, by custom, has sexual relations with upper-caste men, or with just one man, but is not acknowledged as a wife. Limbale is aware of being a bastard child, and I was amazed that I felt a sense of identification with this writer, something that went beyond empathy. I was the child of the rejected wife; I had the sense, back in my childhood, that it is the father who bestows legitimacy. Where did this feeling come from? How, as a female child in a liberal family, did I absorb the defining patriarchal values of a religious culture in my emotional make-up?

The English word 'adultery' is related to 'adulterate', which is defined thus: 'to corrupt, to make something impure by adding an external substance'. The Marathi word *sankar* is similar, it is defined as a 'tumultuous mixture, a medley, farrago, hotchpotch'. Also as: 'A mixed caste or race, a caste proceeding from the promiscuous sexual intercourse of the four tribes in the first instance.' Kaliyug, when the Hindu social order begins to go awry, is an age when *varna-sankar* becomes prevalent.

Only many years later did I realise how deep the emotional currents around rules of caste endogamy and caste patriarchy, run. Transgressing those rules results in children who are the product of *varna-sankar*; their very identity is an anomaly, though other accounts interpret this process as resulting in the formation of new castes or subcastes. It is true that my father's affair, begun when he was fifty and Mrs S in her early forties, did not produce any children, but for a long time I suffered from a mild neurosis about documents that would prove my identity. Subterranean, irrational forces were at work here: the psychological implications for children growing up in a patriarchal family context that is complicated by caste. In our case, the cracks in the structure were a consequence of my father's affair; in 'normal' families, as well as in dysfunctional ones like ours, the rules of caste and patriarchy are absorbed at a deep subconscious level. We need to remember this as we try to eliminate caste from Indian society.

References

[1] Swami Vivekananda, *The Complete Works of Swami Vivekananda*, Vol. 3; Advaita Ashram, 1897, 2013.

[2] George Bühler (trans.), *Manusmriti* (in *Sacred Books of the East*, Vol. 25), 1886.

[3] Pandurang Sadashiv Sane (Sane Guruji), *Shyamchi Aai,* (Marathi) available in English (Pune: Pune Vidyarthi Gruha), 1936.

[4] See the website of Ramakrishna Mission Boys' Home, Singapore: history.

[5] See above, Note 2.

[6] See, for example, my article, 'An Agenda for Gender Politics', *Economic & Political Weekly*, January 1999.

[7] Sharankumar Limbale, *Akkarmashi*, translated into English as *The Outcaste* (New Delhi: Oxford University Press), 2007.

2 Hindutva, Hindu Rashtra & War Hysteria

I returned from a trip to Germany at the end of January 2019. News of the death of close friends, and a vague sense of a worsening political climate, coupled with a bad bout of flu, led to an uneasy awareness of a rising mood of war hysteria around me. This followed the suicide attack that killed over 40 Central Reserve Police Force (CRPF) personnel in Pulwama, Kashmir, on February 14. A wave of aggressive nationalism seemed to be in the ascendant.

With the announcement of the general elections just around the corner, the BJP lost no time in declaring that India needed to vote in a Modi government for another term if the attack in Pulwama were to be given a fitting reply. The *first* response of the ruling regime was to put out posters linking India's military capability with the image of the ruling party: 'India is in safe hands'. 'Push the button with the lotus to ensure India's defence'. In reality, it became clear that despite the fog of disinformation stirred up by a pliant and suddenly jingoistic media, there had been a massive security failure: in September 2019 an internal report by the CRPF, citing serious security lapses, became available to the press.[1] Separately, a digital report revealed another aspect of the February 14 attack: the 40 CRPF jawans belonged primarily to lower-caste communities.

In all, they comprised 19 jawans from Other Backward Classes (or backward castes), seven from Scheduled Castes, five from

Scheduled Tribes, four from upper-caste backgrounds, one high-caste Bengali, three Jat Sikhs, and one Muslim.

A later report specified that nine more jawans had succumbed to their injuries; the media chose not to highlight this news. It was clear that sending so many CRPF personnel in a single convoy on a road with civilian traffic was a huge mistake.

Mourning the CRPF personnel lost in this attack (responsibility for which was soon claimed by a Kashmir-based terrorist group) was, of course, an entirely acceptable reaction. Residential societies in cities held meetings to express their sorrow, wave a few flags, and raise a few slogans. But there was also an air of jingoism, of celebration, of a war-like emotion in the mourning which drowned any feeling of genuine sorrow. News channel anchors and other speakers, dressed in military garb, shouted for revenge. Elsewhere, we had worse: Kashmiri students in different parts of India were physically attacked. A retired senior official of the Indian Air Force, in an interview on a TV news channel, declared that the Pulwama attack should be seen as an act of war by Pakistan, that the country should not accept the claim that terrorist groups working inside India were responsible; India's response should be commensurate with this act of war.

The positions taken by military decision-makers will always be based on a kind of perception and reasoning that is different from those of the government. In a modern democracy, all its institutions have their own jurisdiction, their rules of functioning, and also, ideally, their own culture, so that they can act as checks and balances to each other. The armed forces make a military assessment of the situation, but they await and obey the instructions of the elected government. With Pulwama, however, the concerns of the government, the interests of the ruling party, and the media's release of information all seemed to come together. That is why the bombastic non-official declarations, the government's silence and denials, and the media's whipping up of emotions all fed into a kind of war hysteria. The subversion of the spirit of democracy and of all norms of what we can call decency, fuelled the hysteria. In the process, what was elided was that the security lapses and the intelligence failures demonstrated the callousness of the government with regard to its paramilitary personnel: those thrown into zones of conflict are always the ones who undertake the most dangerous, back-breaking or thankless tasks, whether in war or in daily life in our caste-ridden society.

The military response came on February 26, when Indian Air Force planes entered Pakistani air space, beyond the Line of Control, to strike what were claimed to be 'terrorist training camps'. A few days later, the prime minister, speaking at an official function, declared, 'We have struck fear into the hearts of India's enemies, both internal and external. I repeat, both external and internal. And it is good that there is fear.'[3] So, besides the military action being linked to the ruling dispensation and its clear pointer to the elections, threats were now being issued from the highest quarters to the 'internal enemies' of India—that is, to those that the present government considers its enemies.

The armed forces in India have their own culture; it is secular in the older sense of the word: separation of religion from the state, of which the military is one part. This is different from *sarvadharma samabhaav,* or placing all religions on an equal footing. Pakistan does not have this separation and its armed forces have been in control, without checks and balances, through most of its history. It is bitterly ironic that the very politicians who routinely denounce Pakistan are bent on following Pakistan rather than our own secular Constitution. It is also true that our nationalist emotions are most easily aroused when the enemy in question is Pakistan, rather than say, Sri Lanka or Nepal, for example; for here, both the external and internal enemy is Muslim.

What is nationalism? What is this link between nationalism and war? Between nationalism and religion? Between nationalism and masculinity? Between nationalism, masculinity and gender? How do modern secular democracies institutionalise these links? I pose these questions knowing that the answers will change with time and context, but it is in times like the present that some of these connections, and their implications for our core values like democracy and secularism, become manifest and available for critical contemplation.

War is a reality of the contemporary capitalist world. The arms trade is profitable, and this alone will ensure that, somewhere in the world, wars will be deliberately fomented. Access to and control of natural resources are a major motivation for war, but not a cause that people can be asked to die for. The motive needs to be disguised, which means that wars in today's world are usually built on lies. In 1971, when an India-Pakistan war was being fought I was an undergraduate at Cambridge University. The foreign students in our (all-women's) college were housed in adjacent rooms on what was known in our days as the 'India-Pakistan staircase'. We spoke a common language: Hindustani for us Indian girls, which was close to, but not identical with, 'their' Urdu.

The 1971 war was a full-fledged war. The two countries had not yet acquired nuclear weapons, but we listened to radio broadcasts from both, worried most about the bombing of civilian targets: Karachi and Bombay could both be attacked. However, the camaraderie between us was not disturbed in the least, our anxieties—all of us being far from home—were shared anxieties. And we had a shared culture. Post-Pulwama, there was news of Indian and Pakistani students in Oxford calling for a de-escalation of tensions[4], which brought back memories of my college days, of friendship between Indians and Pakistanis abroad, of a shared longing for peace as we witnessed war.

This is why the war hysteria against Pakistan, the primary manifestation of nationalist sentiment, always seems a little artificial to me. And yet this time the hysteria was different, sounding suspiciously like a Hindu war against a Muslim enemy. In whipping up fury against Muslims as the 'internal enemy', in using the taunt, 'Go to Pakistan' to Muslims and liberals of all religions, and to secularists, the government was clearly using war as a means to secure its domination over its citizens, as the external enemy-internal enemy rhetoric was echoed and adopted by many active and passive supporters of Hindutva. Pacifism, in this scheme of things, was equated with 'anti-nationalism'.

Feminists have opposed war because of what happens to innocent men, women and children in zones of conflict, and because women face the consequences of wars started by men: poverty, following the death of the main breadwinner; destruction of homes and livelihoods; injuries and prolonged sickness among survivors. Indian feminists have protested the use of brute force by the armed forces, especially against women in Kashmir and the north-east. Lately, they have also questioned the very rationale of territorial aggression, and of ethnic nationalism, often a potent motivation.[5]

On the other hand, nearer home, the history of the RSS and its Hindutva project has always encouraged women, to not so much play a supportive role in actual wars, but to call up the masculine spirit of aggression against 'external and internal enemies'. We saw this in the inflammatory language of Sadhvi Rithambhara at the time of L.K. Advani's rath yatra in the late 1980s, culminating in the demolition of the Babri Masjid in 1992. Later, too, the BJP and its sister associations managed to recruit many women into their project of war against the 'external and internal' enemies, and into acts of extreme violence, especially in Gujarat in 2002, and elsewhere, in Uttar Pradesh, over the next two decades.

Like the Nazis in Germany in the 1930s, Hindutvavadis of today advocate and justify the most brutal and inhuman violence against the 'internal enemy' as a means of restoring a wounded nationalist pride. Defeat in the First World War, a lag in economic development, the sense of being, at best, a third-rate imperialist power, fed into the sentiments that led many Germans to support the Nazis who, we should remember, came to power through the democratic process. For Hindus, a history of conquest by foreign powers, in which Mughal rule somehow seems more ignominious than colonial rule by the British, nurses a similar grievance.

Commercial considerations often outweigh nationalist ones in the contemporary world. When I visited Vietnam in late 2019, it was disconcerting to find that the war of liberation from US occupation, which had inspired us in the 1970s, was being described merely as a war for the reunification of the country. The need to woo American tourists, and perhaps the different dreams of a younger generation, have blunted nationalist articulation even in exhibitions that recount the history of the war, which was indeed a heroic war. The tragedy is that the markets of today, such as the markets generated by the huge spread of social media across the globe and across social strata, do not hesitate, directly or indirectly, to use the politics of hatred to enhance their reach. Hindutva, for example, has generated corporate support; and the use of social media to promote communal hatred, with all its masculinist trappings, is enhanced by the policies and algorithms used by the capitalist corporates running social media platforms.

In the present atmosphere of politicised jingoism in India, pacifism, or any expression of a yearning for peace is seen not only as emasculated and weak, but—a new term made popular by the media and some government spokesmen (and spokeswomen)—anti-national. It was in 2016 that a video showing Gurmehar Kaur, aged 21, the daughter of an army captain who was killed in the Kargil war, went viral on social media. In it, she holds up a placard saying, 'Pakistan didn't kill my father, War did.' She speaks of how it felt to have lost her father at the age of two, saying that for some time she hated Pakistanis and all Muslims. She then holds up more placards calling for an end to state-sponsored terrorism, state-sponsored spying, and state-sponsored hatred.[6]

Gurmehar Kaur faced severe trolling on social media; she was called an anti-national, even received rape threats, which have become common currency for certain kinds of supporters of the Modi government. This really upset me. The girl was young, she had lost her father, she was expressing her pain, she had moved away from anger and hatred to a yearning for peace. What kind of mindset could condemn her in such an insensitive manner? I said so on a WhatsApp group of cousins, people I know well, and was surprised that no one agreed with me.

The same group, or some members of it, have been calling for a boycott of Chinese goods in response to the Chinese veto in the United Nations Security Council of India's motion to have Jaish-e-Mohammad chief, Masood Azhar, declared a global terrorist. This is a symptom of the currently prevalent feeling of being obliged to demonstrate one's nationalism through some sort of action. Over the last few years, this has sometimes taken on aggressive forms, with 'nationalism vigilantes' demanding that one should say 'Bharat Mata ki Jai' when asked to do so. The icons of nationalism are increasingly confused with Hindu icons. Several scholars have written about the 'Mother India' figure painted by Abanindranath Tagore—an ascetic figure holding a book, prayer beads, a sheaf of grain, and a piece of white cloth in her four hands;[7] a figure having at least some aspects of inclusiveness. By 2016 this had given way to a much more visibly upper-caste, somewhat pugnacious woman mounted on a lion, against the background of a map of India and the national flag. Competition has recently arisen among state governments about who raises the tallest national flag. When I visited Raipur in 2015, I was taken aback by the sight of the huge Indian flag fluttering in the centre of this capital city of Chhattisgarh. Is this 'bigger is better' nationalism not overtly masculinist in its symbolism, and in its celebration of Bharat Mata?

While writing this section I first tried to position myself in relation to the rapidly evolving events around me, as we neared the end of a five-year term for a government which had, from the beginning, posed as the defender of 'true' nationalism. The attacks in Pathankot in January 2016, Uri in September 2016, and Pulwama in February 2019, were all occasions for the heightening of a militant nationalist rhetoric, in which the present regime was projected as having a 'muscular' and emphatic approach to Pakistan-sponsored terrorism, led by a prime minister with a '56-inch chest'. It was an aggressive masculinist discourse, and was lapped up eagerly by many Indian women. The Hindu nationalist rhetoric has continued since then, and the Pulwama terror attack triggered a new wave of belligerent Hindu nationalist sentiment. It was an effective ploy, however cynical and manipulative it might have appeared to critics of the ruling regime.

The Maratha agitation of recent years in Maharashtra is not exactly part of the Hindutva current, but it has seen women sporting turbans and carrying flags, celebrating the military legacy of the 17th century Maratha king, Chhatrapati Shivaji, who fought both the Mughals and the British. Thankfully, this was a symbolic rather than an actual display of women's support for the masculine penchant for war, but it has been equally insensitive to women's actual needs and their attempts to attain real freedom. Its target is Dalits rather than Muslims. Hindu militancy finds its most aggressive expression in positioning itself against Muslims; the Maratha andolan appeals to caste sentiments of injustice, while Marathas have always been firmly ensconced in positions of power in Maharashtra, ever since the state was formed in 1960. What the two have in common is the pathetic falsehood of a dominant community perceiving itself as the victim.

I have written above about how I, as an Indian citizen who has lived abroad, witnessed (though at a distance) the impact of different wars; how, as a woman, I have sensed the machismo and misogyny that are an essential part of this rhetoric and public sentiment; how as a Hindu by birth, I shrink from the shrill, exclusionary, hate-filled version of Hinduism that is being expressed. But Hinduism, Hindutva nationalism and war are much more deep-rooted, complex and traumatic than my response to it, given that I was born after Partition and independence. To understand it more fully we have to go into this country's history.

Those of us who were born soon after India became independent grew up in a country where a secular temper was being painstakingly cultivated. Secular institutions had to be *built*, and a secular temper inculcated: in the armed forces, in education, in the field of culture. The liberal model of higher education, as well as scientific research, under attack today from right-wing forces, was a part of this effort. The films of that era and their music took up many themes relevant to this project, now described as Nehruvian, and been subject to criticism from various quarters in the last couple of decades. The critique from a neo-liberal paradigm talks of too much government interference in economic matters: the so-called mixed economy approach did not boost technological innovation, expand the manufacturing sector or create jobs on a large scale. Another criticism by feminists, Dalit groups and Ambedkarites, among others, is that the excessive power placed in the hands of a bureaucracy, dominated by an implicitly Brahmanical, patriarchal mindset, reproduced the social inequalities and caste-gender hierarchies inherent to our society.

But these and other reservations about the Nehruvian era have been drowned by the vociferous claim made by right-wing Hindutva forces that the Jawaharlal Nehru regime 'appeased' Muslims in India and did not exhibit sufficient assertion/aggression in its foreign policy, especially with regard to Pakistan and China. The tendency of even the top-rung leaders of the BJP to routinely speak of 'seventy years of misrule under the Nehru dynasty' muddies the waters and confuses us as to what exactly he is being blamed for.

However, in order to think of Nehru as the leader of a team that shaped the secular mould and its institutions in independent India, we need to revert to the situation as it was before independence.

Hindu nationalism is a term used by Dr B.R. Ambedkar in his *Thoughts on Pakistan*,[8] written in 1946, a starkly realistic assessment of the arguments for and against the partition of India. Identifying neither with the Muslim nor the Hindu community, he acknowledged the deep-rooted bitterness and mistrust between the two, and pointed out the administrative, military and political implications of this for the future of an India independent of British rule. He acknowledged that Muslims had been belligerent and aggressive in demanding certain political concessions and a substantial share in representation on various administrative bodies. But he also quoted at length from V.D. Savarkar to argue that these demands were a response to an aggressive pursuit of majoritarian domination by the Hindus. So, rather than blame the British for a policy of 'divide and rule' (though he did not deny that this was a factor) he demonstrated that the existing divisions were really deep, and probably unmanageable, in an undivided India. He showed, quoting official records, that the army of the North

West Frontier Province and Punjab was, in 1930, staffed by a majority of Muslims; in later decades, he found that the British did not release data on the social composition of the armed forces. The domination of military elites in Pakistan is a phenomenon whose base was laid by the British, perhaps in an attempt to counter the rise of Hindu nationalist forces in the freedom struggle.

As elsewhere, in this book, too, Ambedkar was a fierce critic of Gandhi's style of politics, especially his reliance on personal charisma and passive coercion through his fasts and silences. He was critical of the way Gandhi inducted Muslims into the Congress by espousing the cause of Khilafat; but above all, this little book underlined the realities of the 'Hindu-Muslim problem' in undivided India. There were Hindu nationalists both inside and outside the Indian National Congress who dreamt of, and spoke and wrote about, Akhand Bharat, an undivided Hindu nation, where Muslims and Christians would be expected to subjugate themselves to a Hindu religious state. Muslim leaders responded by making demands for sweeping concessions, for representation in government, and by pushing their agenda aggressively. Ambedkar implied that the available alternatives to Partition were unworkable.

Even after large chunks of territory and population were ceded to Pakistan on the north-western and eastern borders of the new Indian nation, India continued to retain a large Muslim population. I remember my father saying that India's policy with regard to two of its largest princely states was inconsistent: when Kashmir's Hindu king opted to remain in the Indian union, its largely Muslim population was denied a referendum and the state acceded to India; but when the Nizam of Hyderabad resisted absorption, the Indian army was moved in against his feudal force, the Razakars, and the state was brought into the Union of India by force. Nobody talks about the thousands of innocent Muslims who were killed in Hyderabad in 1948 during the Indian military action. In Aurangabad, capital of Marathwada, the liberation of Marathwada from the Nizam and his Razakars is celebrated every year on September 17, but in all the years that I lived there, no one ever mentioned this massacre in my presence. A.G. Noorani has written about it, with supporting references, in *The Destruction of Hyderabad*.[9] The Hindu nationalism that Ambedkar spoke of produces many such silences, even so many years down the line. The silence in this case feeds the resentment among Muslims, a fertile ground for the fundamentalist sentiments which are now visible among some citizens of cities like Aurangabad.

Hindutva nationalism vs secularism

Our Constitution has declared India to be a secular, democratic republic. Muslims and Christians are recognised as 'minorities', and like every other religious grouping, allowed to have their own personal laws and religious educational institutions. Sikhs, Jains and Buddhists, also minorities, are nevertheless considered to be part of the Hindu community. Parsis are distinct from all the above.

Post-Partition, assurances to Muslims became necessary not just because the maulanas demanded them, but because as a secular nation, India had to clearly announce itself as different from the Islamic nation of Pakistan; and also because there were still voices, even within the Indian National Congress, that called for a Hindu rashtra. The strongest organisation representing these sentiments, the Rashtriya Swayamsevak Sangh, was banned after the assassination of Gandhi, but it became legal and openly active again when Indira Gandhi's Emergency was lifted in 1977. Nehru, a liberal thinker in his individual capacity, was mindful of the other meaning of the word 'secular', that of separation of state and religion, but because Hinduism sanctifies the hierarchical and exclusionary practice of caste, it was necessary to provide affirmative action to those groups whose exclusion was most extreme.

Gradually, religion came to dominate politics. Sunil Khilnani, in his fascinating book, *The Idea of India*,[10] argues that democracy for most Indians soon came to mean electoral politics alone. Elections in independent India became festive occasions, something that Indians embraced with enthusiasm. As I had grown up outside India, I found it strange that even the most insignificant election, say, to a post in some association which carried no real power or monetary benefit, still called forth a great deal of energy in self-presentation and lobbying within the constituency. It is not surprising, then, that elections are fought in terms of vote-banks, that gods are invoked and candidates sent to canvass with large red tilaks on their foreheads, and that politicians of all stripes consult their favourite godmen for the best path to victory.

Despite seventy years of independence and a constitutionally democratic, secular state, Hindu nationalism has remained alive and well, and not only in extremist organisations like the RSS. Our deeply flawed democracy rumbles on, the secularism of its institutions being gradually eroded over time.

I had my own experience of how religion enters secular institutions on two occasions, when I was warden of a university hostel for women students, during my tenure as a teacher in Aurangabad. The first was in 1989. Just before the Ganesh festival, which occurs in the monsoon month of Bhadrapada, some girls expressed a desire to instal a Ganesh murti in the entrance lobby of the hostel. (This was already common practice in many colleges in Maharashtra.) I called a meeting and explained that the hostel was part of a public institution funded by the secular Indian state, and that girls of different faiths were living in it; students were free to instal Ganesh murtis in their rooms if their roommates did not object. This was accepted, maybe with a little reluctance, but no protest. However, when I became warden again in the year 2000, the practice of installing a Ganesh idol in the main shared space of the hostel was already well established. All I could do was to warn the girls collecting funds for the accompanying worship, feasting and celebrations, that they were not to make subscription compulsory; only those who wanted to contribute should do so. Some Dalit students later met me and thanked me for this.

Thus, Hindu majoritarianism in India's public life was a growing presence once the first euphoria of independence had worn off; but even so, after the Modi-led BJP government came to power in May 2014, this tendency has been entrenched more systematically. Muslims have been explicitly targeted, as have Dalits, but there has not been a comparable anti-Dalit rhetoric; on the contrary, the pretence that Dalits are a part of the Hindu fold (despite converting to Buddhism) and are better-off that way, has gained ground. The beef ban, the lynching of cattle traders, the shrill rhetoric against inter-religious marriages turning violent, with terms like 'love jihad' and 'ghar wapsi', have created an atmosphere of impunity for those who attack Muslims on any pretext. And so we now have a lethal mixture of war hysteria and enmity towards Muslims in our own nation, citizens, like every other Indian, of a secular republic.

Hindutva, Hinduism, and war

The term 'Hindutva' was coined by V.D. Savarkar to denote a militant Hinduism asserting the need for a modern Hindu nation. While Hinduism, however we understand the term, continues to be the private faith of a majority of Indians, politicians of the right are vigorously engaged in trying to conflate Hinduism with Hindutva. We have discussed above how Hindutva tries to whip up war hysteria and a supposedly nationalist sentiment against Pakistan and Muslim citizens of India. I have not talked about the more recent steps taken in implementing the Hindutva project of building a Hindu rashtra, such as the abrogation of Article 370 of the Constitution in Kashmir, nor of the Citizenship Amendment Act, the National Register of Citizens, or the proposed National Population Register, which have evoked widespread protest among Hindus and Muslims, students, women, and the general public.

The Hindutva project aims its appeal at ordinary Hindus. Some Hindu believers say that the Hindutva being propagated today by the ruling party and its followers is not the Hinduism they believe in. But what do the sacred texts of Hinduism have to say about war? We cannot expect them to have anything to say about nationalism, which is a modern concept. But, after all, the *Bhagavad Gita*, the sacred text that Hindus swear on when they take oath in court, is part of the narrative of the *Mahabharata,* and consists of a conversation in which Krishna persuades the reluctant prince, Arjuna, to go to war against his close relatives. There is no wrong in fighting a righteous war, he is told, as long as one is detached from its consequences and has no desire for the fruits of war. Killing one's enemy is not a sin, because one kills only the body and not the soul, or atman. The Kshatriya's dharma is to fight:[11]

> 30. This dweller in the body of everyone is eternal and indestructible. O Bharata: therefore thou shouldst not grieve for any creature.
>
> 31. Further, looking to thine own law of action thou shouldst not tremble; there is no greater good for the Kshatriya than righteous battle.

> 32. When such a battle comes to them of itself like the open gate of heaven, happy are the Kshatriyas then.
>
> 33. But if thou dost not this battle for the right, then hast thou abandoned thy duty and virtue and thy glory, and sin shall be thy portion.
>
> 34. Besides, men will recount thy perpetual disgrace, and to one in noble station, dishonour is worse than death.

This is advice to a prince, a Kshatriya male; the broader message to Hindus is, do the duty assigned to you by your status at birth without seeking reward (or, at least, without seeking it in this birth). The war being fought here is not a war against an external enemy, an invader or an oppressor; it is a fratricidal war. Of course, the holy books of Hinduism, as in all religions, are composed in a historical era previous to the present and so the pretexts and goals of war are bound to be different from modern times. The *Gita* preaches detachment from the fruits of one's actions while exhorting Arjun—and, by extension, all Hindus—to undertake that action appropriate to one's given place in the social order, caste- and gender-wise.

What does the message of the *Gita* have to do with today's Hindu nationalist war mania? For one thing, today the 'enemy' is identified as Muslim—whether it is Pakistan or Indian Muslims in general (more specifically, Muslim men), who are routinely accused of cow slaughtering, 'love jihad' or terrorism. Attacking Muslims becomes a 'religious' act for Hindus. The claim of the 'spiritualism' of Indians, based on the *Gita*'s message of detachment from the fruits of one's actions, was opposed to the materialism of the British, notoriously 'a nation of shopkeepers'. There were works of literature that strongly articulated these claims, one of the most famous being Bankim Chandra Chattopadhyay's Bengali novel, *Anandmath.* The novel was written in 1882, before the 1905 partition of Bengal, which saw an upsurge of Hindu nationalism against the British. It accords a central place to the patriotic song, Vande Mataram, which today's Hindutva forces propose as the national anthem, an alternative to Jana Gana Mana. It is interesting that present-day Hindutva singles out the song as a possible anthem for a Hindu rashtra, but does not talk much about the novel itself, even though it paints a glorified picture of Hindu nationalism. One reason for this may be that the novel does not posit Muslims as the enemy; it pivots around the heroic deeds of a group of *Hindu* rebels, and all the leaders are identified as upper-caste, either Brahmin or Kshatriya. Muslims, Sikhs and Christians are mentioned (but are never visible), standing together in the fight for freedom from British rule, and firmly under Hindu leadership. This is an imagined India where Hindu (read twice-born Hindu) leadership is never disputed.

The Hindu model of 'unselfish militancy' that Basanta Koomar Roy refers to in his introduction to the English translation of the novel, contains many elements that will be familiar to anyone who follows the politics of the RSS and the Bharatiya Janata Party. A glorification of the marital bond in which the high-caste, high-minded wife subordinates herself to her husband's mission, with the man freeing himself from the constraints of the same bond for a higher mission, also glorified. Occasionally, we even have a woman who dresses like a man and performs heroic deeds, but ultimately she accepts her primary identity as a wife. Or, a wife may poison herself and her child so that they are not a burden to her rebel soldier husband. Desire for a woman, even 'excessive' attachment to one's wife and child, are emotions that weaken a man. The bearded guru is another central figure: a Brahmin ascetic who is the source of wisdom and strategy, and has an ashram which provides shelter and sattvik food to rebels in hiding.

What we find in the novel is a response to the Orientalist depiction of the Indian (read Hindu) male as weak and lazy, cowardly, and unmanly. The twice-born freedom fighters, referred to as the Children (of Bharat Mata, or the Motherland) manage to defeat the British in battle; but a casteist message is repeated in several places. The 'sepoys' are the Indian traitors, the poor pariahs, and perhaps Muslims, who join the army of the invaders. When famine ravages the countryside, it is the lower castes and jungle-dwellers who turn to bestiality. These messages are peppered throughout the narrative, without great emphasis, as its main objective is to portray the upper-caste Hindu militant, with his creed of non-attachment to the fruits of his actions, as the true son of Bharat Mata.

"*You have renounced your families. But have you been able to free yourself from the ties of love and affection?... We do not pretend to be above all attachment. We simply observe the sanctity of our vows.*"[12]

What I learn from my reading of *Anandmath* is that a feeling of inferiority (chiefly with respect to the British) underlies the hate speech and masculinist posturing that characterise Hindutva politics. The sanctity of the Hindu family, with its patriarchal structure and its awareness of caste identity, is to be preserved, even though the war of independence may throw everything into turmoil.

The antagonism towards Muslims that characterises the ideology of Hindu fundamentalist groups like the RSS, the Hindu Mahasabha and, lately, the Vishva Hindu Parishad began to take substantive form only after the 1905 partition of Bengal, which the Hindutva leadership feared would create a Muslim-dominated province. The unity of Bengal was restored in 1911 after massive protests, but it was after Muslims began demanding adequate political representation in the administrative reorganisation and self-governance arrangements proposed by the British, that they became clearly identified as the 'enemy'. Of course, there was always tension between Hindus and Muslims, and communal riots did take place from time to time; but there is some substance in the claim that these tensions were exacerbated by British policy.

Today, the message of Hindutva is more complicated: Hindus are a peaceful people because we have never invaded another country; but 'pseudo-secularists' have been soft on our enemies (read Muslims, outside and within the country) and a new militant Hinduism will defend itself aggressively. We see a shoring up of a nationalism based on exclusion, which is why the comparison with the Nazis (*National*

Socialists, lest we forget) is valid. It is a nationalism *defined* by the fact that some citizens are less equal than others. The protests against the Citizenship Amendment Act of 2019 have been a reaction to the conversion of this view of nationalism into law, but there are other views of the nation. What is important is that for nationalism in a nation that is not only diverse but structured by inequality, contesting views of the nation and of patriotic struggles must be allowed free expression.

At the beginning of 2018, a mass celebration of what Dalits see as a battle validating their courage and military prowess, became the occasion not just for anti-Dalit violence, but for a whole programme of misrepresentation and accusation, not to mention arrests, over the question of nationalism. On January 1, 2018, hundreds of thousands of Dalits gathered in the village of Koregaon, on the river Bhima near Pune, to commemorate a battle in which a small number of Mahars and other 'low caste' soldiers fought with the British army against a huge contingent of the Peshwas, ruling from Pune. This regime, with a Maratha king on the throne, was nevertheless run by a Brahmin elite that stepped up cruel and humiliating practices against those deemed untouchable in the caste hierarchy. Dalits see the battle of Bhima-Koregaon as triggering the collapse of Peshwa rule; those who died in battle are venerated as martyrs. Dr B.R. Ambedkar visited the memorial in 1927 and revived this history, since when it has become a site of assertion by the Dalits who were, however, seen as being 'anti-national' because their heroes had fought alongside the British. January 1, 2018, was the 200th anniversary of the battle, and the numbers that congregated in Koregaon were even larger than usual. A physical attack on the crowd was allegedly led by two Brahmin provocateurs, who have not been arrested till date. Dalit protests broke out over the incident and were quickly quelled, with a number of protesters being arrested. Over the next few months, several left-wing activists were charge-sheeted in connection with this incident and some were jailed.[13]

The debate over the Bhima-Koregaon gathering of January 2018 and its aftermath has brought into public discourse the idea that the history of nation-formation is many-layered, and can have different meanings for different sections of society—an inclusive conception of citizenship of the nation must recognise and respect these different narratives. As the ruling regime tries to push the alternative conception of a Hindu Rashtra, we must remember, first, that a secular vision of India was consciously and laboriously articulated and built against the background of the violence and bitterness that accompanied Partition. Second, that this vision is sustainable only if it is also open to contestation and emerging challenges in the contemporary context, especially from marginalised and long-silenced voices. The Constitution adopted by the Indian Union in 1950 enshrines both these principles; defending our secular institutions may inevitably mean rebuilding them from the foundations.

Defending the Constitution implies defending a vision of India that our founding fathers and mothers shared, and fought for. Our democratic institutions are the scaffolding that holds everything together. Our traditions are not monoliths, they are shaped by our everyday conduct, by facing the problems of the present with the intelligence gained from the past. As a citizen of India and as a woman, I want a modern, egalitarian, creative and prosperous India, that ensures dignity to every woman, man and child, based on the rich natural wealth of our land and our symbiosis with its ecology.

That India is not a Hindu Rashtra.

References

[1] 'Pulwama Terror Attack Preceded by "Massive Intelligence Failure", Finds CRPF Report', https://thewire.in/security, September 6, 2019.

[2] 'Urban upper-castes driving Hindutva nationalism have little representation among Pulwama's slain jawans', https://caravanmagazine.in/caste/, February 21, 2019.

[3] 'The Daily Fix: By attacking "internal enemies", Modi government is channeling repressive regimes', https://scroll.in/, March 6, 2019.

[4] 'Indian and Pakistani students at Oxford say "No" to war', https://timesofindia.indiatimes.com/world/south-asia, March 5, 2019.

[5] There are many references. Two recent books, one from the US and one from India, are: Laura Sjoberg, *Gendering Global Conflict: Toward a Feminist Theory of War* (New York: Columbia University Press), 2016, and Ritu Menon (ed.), *No Woman's Land: Women from Pakistan, India and Bangladesh Write on the Partition of India* (New Delhi: Women Unlimited), 2004, 2017.

[6] See note in Chapter 1.

[7] See Charu Gupta, 'The Icon of Mother in Late Colonial North India: "Bharat Mata", "Matri Bhasha" and "Gau Mata"', *Economic & Political Weekly*, November 10–16, 2001.

[8] *Thoughts on Pakistan* was first published in 1946. It appears in Volume 8 of his *Writings and Speeches*, published by the Government of Maharashtra, 1990, 2014.

[9] A.J. Noorani, *The Destruction of Hyderabad* (New Delhi: Tulika Books), 2013.

[10] Sunil Khilnani, *The Idea of India* (New Delhi: Penguin India), 2004.

[11] I used the Internet, looking up the *Bhagvad Gita*; the quotes are from an English translation by Aurobindo Ghose. This is also available in print, edited by Anirban Roy, Shri Aurobindo Ashram Trust, Pondicherry.

[12] Bankim Chandra Chattopadhyay, *Anandmath*, translated with an introduction by Basanta Koomar Roy, who says that the novel rejuvenated the Bengali language.

[13] See, for example, Anand Teltumbde, *Hindutva and Dalits: Perspectives for Understanding Communal Praxis* (New Delhi: Sage India), 2020.

3 Hinduism and Other Religions

I have been underlining throughout this monograph, from the very first chapter, that my rejection of Hinduism is a rejection not only of the extreme and aggressive version of political Hinduism that has been espoused and promoted by the government and the Bharatiya Janata Party in power over the last three decades or so, but a rejection of Hinduism as it continues to be practised in daily life in modern India, especially of the caste hierarchy and patriarchy that are inherent to it. The most aggressive version of Hindutva that makes us face new horrors every day, builds on the *fundamentally exclusive and hierarchical nature* of Hinduism, a religion that is professed by the majority of Indians.

I have also stated earlier that I am an atheist, but I am not a militant atheist. I respect and empathise with many people, including many Hindus, who are genuinely religious. Atheism apart, I have never seriously thought of taking to any other religion, though I spent two years in the intensely Roman Catholic atmosphere of a girls' boarding school of the Loreto sorority. While I was a student in Cambridge, some of my closest friends were Jewish, and we often remarked on how Indian families and Jewish families resembled each other. My brother, Sudhir, whom I was close to, flirted for some time with the idea of converting to Islam. Nobody in our family took this very seriously, though earlier, when a cousin of Sudhir's age had considered becoming a Christian, his parents and other relatives were horrified.

I have, however, two major concerns in writing *this* chapter. One is to show how my encounters with other religions brought home to me that, while they all had patriarchal values at their core, especially with regard to marriage and the family, religions other than Hinduism had some notion of the equality of human beings before one's creator; this became the basis for a universal ethics, and the possibility of deriving one's personal morality from a faith that regards all human beings as equal in some sense.

My second concern has to do with the specific ways in which the current avatar of Hinduism views other religions, and how the present government, with its increasingly overt project of bringing about a Hindu Rashtra, proposes to deal with people, especially Indian citizens, of other faiths. This is not a new project. Its basic elements can be found in the publications of the Rashtriya Swayamsevak Sangh (RSS) and its sister organisations dating back to the 1920s.

All religions are fundamentally patriarchal, their value systems are based on patriarchal social structures. The meaning of the word patriarchy has changed somewhat in the decades after feminist scholars lifted it from its anthropological context and applied it to modern society. The original meaning would apply to a structure headed by a **patriarch**, who is the male head of a family, household, or tribal line; today, a widely accepted definition of patriarchy would be something like the following: **Patriarchy** is a social system in which men hold primary power and predominate in roles of political leadership, moral authority, social privilege and control of property. It extends beyond the family or kinship group, to society as a whole.

Hinduism: society in the image of family

The family in contemporary India remains the central social institution in which patriarchal relationships and values are nurtured. This is even more so in the case of Hindu families in modern times, compared to other religious communities, whether it be the extended multi-generational family or the nuclear family. Relationships outside the family, in the workplace or in civil and political life, are spoken of, and thought of, in terms of relationships within the family. So, we have the description of the government as 'mai-baap sarkar', a term that was applied to the British government in colonial times, as well as to the democratically elected government in independent India. (The RSS constellation of organisations is similarly characterised as the Sangh Parivar, with the RSS as the parent, the *pater familias*.) This has coloured the attitude of people, especially the poor, towards the claiming of their entitlements from the welfare programmes of the state, their rights to land, water, natural resources, in general; in short, to their right to a life of dignity. Our educational institutions also deploy the ideology and language of the family. I used to tell my students in a women's studies class: 'If a young male college student is seen misbehaving with a female classmate, he is asked how he would feel if this happened to his sister.

He will not be told that it is unacceptable because he should treat all women with respect, or that the young woman is a college student like himself. How does his sister come into it?' It is the biological family analogy that is always invoked, or the wider family: the caste.

Ambedkar has rightly observed that,

> Caste has made public opinion impossible. A Hindu's public is his caste. His responsibility is only to his caste. His loyalty is restricted to his caste. Virtue has become caste-ridden and morality has become caste-bound.

This is one sense of what we mean when we say that Hindu society is ordered as a caste patriarchy: all relationships are modelled after relationships within the patriarchal family, and the only unit wider than the family that is truly recognised in the Hindu ethical world, is the caste. So, the patriarch is primarily the *pater familias*, and by extension, the male caste elder. Law is the law of the caste panchayat, a law that discriminates between boys and girls, young men and young women, and uses older women to enforce the rules that empower them only through their relationship with men.

The Judaeo-Christian, or more broadly the Abrahamic religions (Judaism, Christianity and Islam) are in fact different in this respect. The term Abrahamic implies not only monotheism, with a God who is unequivocally a He, but also great patriarchal figures who tower over society and mankind: Abraham, Moses, Jesus, and Mohammed. The prophets of the Old Testament are recognised by all three religions. Islam recognises the prophets who came before Mohammed Paighambar, after whom there will be no other prophet. Thus, it is possible in these religions to talk of moral laws for all mankind, of a *universal* ethics, even though that ethics, too, is patriarchal in the last instance. In Hinduism, on the other hand, there is dharma, which is always determined by one's social status and one's gender. The modern, liberal-democratic principle of all citizens being equal before the law, resonates with the religions that profess all men (yes, men) to be equal before God. In Hinduism, dharma for the Brahmin is not the same as dharma for the Shudra, who is born to serve others; or for the Dalit, who is an outcaste because he does those jobs for society which religion has deemed polluting. This is why our liberal-democratic principles remain academic; they do not enter our hearts. In India and in South Asia more generally, Muslims, Sikhs and Christians also adopt rules of endogamy similar to those followed by Hindus with their caste system, but here it is not sanctioned by religion, it is a social practice that has evolved over time.

Hindutva, with its current project of forging a majoritarian consensus for the establishment of a Hindu Rashtra, has become increasingly aggressive towards other religions. Even in modern India, Hinduism earlier had a relationship of both tolerance and intolerance, of openness and co-option, vis-à-vis other religions. In fact, it has never been a proselytising religion because it does not allow conversion. You have to be a born a Hindu, which means you are always already assigned to a particular caste at birth. This feature of Hinduism becomes the pretext for an expressed anxiety about the dwindling numbers of Hindus: the danger of conversion by Dalits to Christianity or Islam is ever present. A Hindu can 'lose caste' through pollution, marriage or conversion. New converts to the Hindu fold are unthinkable, for what caste would they be placed in? Ghar wapsi, or homecoming, for recent converts from Hinduism is easier, because they can be placed right back in the caste they converted from.

My encounter with Christianity

I came into contact with Christianity, and I suppose its ethical principles, at an early age. By the time I started at a Catholic convent boarding school in Shimla at the age of eleven, my mind was a fertile ground for receiving the significant amount of religious material we were exposed to. Compulsory attendance at Mass every Sunday when we listened to the litany in Latin; a daily half-hour in the chapel for rosary, when non-Christian girls were allowed to bring their own prayer books; hymn singing, and frequent doses of what was right and wrong. There was also the constant evocation of the Virgin Mary, typical of Roman Catholicism: we were told that God was merciful, but the Mother of God was even more understanding of our weak and sinful selves, as long as we tried sincerely to be better. There were paintings on the chapel wall depicting the Stations of the Cross, or the significant events that took place as Jesus Christ carried his cross to his own crucifixion. The Bible has lots of fascinating stories, and these were what seduced us rather than any overt attempts at conversion. There were Hindu, Muslim and Sikh girls in the school, and I remember that they were allowed to practise their religion in small ways, keeping images or pictures of their gods in their dormitory cupboards. I personally carried no such baggage from my home.

I recall that among my closest friends were a Sikh girl with short hair, a Maharashtrian who never tired of telling us that she was the child of a marriage between a Rajput father and a Maratha mother (much later, she carried out a brave and spectacular rebellion by running away to get married), and a Muslim. I was also friends with a Roman Catholic girl who was two years senior to me, the only one I am still in touch with. The heavy dose of Roman Catholic Christianity certainly influenced us, since we were anyway at an impressionable age; some girls even declared that they wanted to become nuns, skipping over the fact that they would have to convert to Christianity first.

Since the Loreto Convent string of schools and colleges was mainly concentrated in Bengal, we had, besides a short summer break, Puja holidays during Durga Puja, the nine days leading up to Dussehra that are observed in different ways in different regions of India. I did not at that time have any inkling of what this festival was all about. Most of the girls went home to their families, but since my family was abroad and too far away for a short trip, I stayed back at school. There was often a retreat during that period, participation in which was voluntary. Retreats were an opportunity for me to indulge my appetite for out-of-syllabus reading.

I treasure all this as something I gained from Christianity; but later in life I experienced a sense of the spiritual in many places of worship: temples, Buddhist viharas, gurudwaras, mosques and churches. When I was a student in England, I once had a strong pang of nostalgia when an image of the stone steps of a temple, slightly damp, with scattered flowers and the sound of bells, crossed my mind. Not the image of a deity. Many religious sites are located in beautiful surroundings, and I, as an atheist, am not a stranger to the sense of the mystical that one experiences there.

Personally, I was not impacted by my school, a deeply Christian educational establishment, as an institution aiming to convert Hindus. Rather, it gave me a many-sided understanding of the Christian, or more accurately, the Roman Catholic, faith. This is something I consider to be an enriching part of my education. I do not recall any anxiety about or resistance to the compulsory participation in certain Christian daily observances, even among the girls who came from a more Hindu background than I did.

Christianity, unlike Hinduism, is well-known as a proselytising religion; this is part of India's colonial history. We know that Christian missionaries opened schools that initially admitted children from the 'lower' castes; this was the earliest opportunity for such children to acquire an education. We also know that some of these missionary schools closed their doors to 'untouchable' children when upper-caste parents threatened to take their wards out. The Christian mission in India, as well as the government administration, constantly consulted, always negotiated and compromised with the Brahmanical establishment, the priests and scholars. This is the face of Christianity that we generally see in India; a much more violent and frightening Christianity is an indelible part of world history.

Hinduism, Hindutva and Christianity

In the present phase of Hindutva nationalism, Christians engaged in charitable works are placed under suspicion, accused of trying to convert poor Hindus, especially Adivasis and Dalits. This is presented as their primary, clandestine activity. In fact, there are still a large number of hospitals and schools run by various church organisations in India, mostly missionary orders, which have been here for a long time, and whose main arenas are health and education. Social reformers in the 19th century, from Jotirao Phule to M G Ranade, found Christian missionaries to be useful collaborators in the task of spreading liberal ideas and reform in education, and in delivering medical services to society. In Phule's concept of Nirmik or Creator, we see the influence of the Abrahamic concept of God as Creator, with all created human beings equal before Him. There was an openness to certain Christian ideas, as in the writings of Pandita Ramabai, the formidable social reformer who had a difficult childhood during which her father taught her the Sanskrit texts, breaking a sacred Hindu tradition. Ramabai later converted to Christianity, although she had problems with the Christian faith, too (as revealed in a published collection of her letters), expressing her doubts and misgivings, and her arguments with the sisters she was in contact with.

It was opposition from orthodox Brahmins, the early forerunners of the Hindutva ideologues of the late 20th and 21st centuries, who eventually pressurised M G Ranade into breaking ties with Pandita Ramabai. Today's Hindutva can be described as 'political Hinduism', echoing Martin Kramer; fundamentalists try to unite the proponents of their religion, whether Islam, Christianity, Hinduism, or even Buddhism against an Other of other religions, who is then constructed as the enemy. Hindutva in the contemporary context is thus a proselytising ideology, even if Hinduism is not. We see 'political Hinduism' today trying to 'convert' those people—the majority in our variegated nation, who follow Hindu religious practices and who enter their religion as Hindu on official forms—into a homogenised community, one that believes that it has been the victim of Muslim violence in the past and is threatened by it in the present.

Hindutva and the construction of the Muslim as enemy

The transformation here requires the rewriting of history and a construction of present-day Muslims as having certain characteristics that are contemptible, dangerous and inferior. This constructed image of the Muslim, which is often self-contradictory, finds expression in the speeches of leaders of the present ruling party; in the WhatsApp, Twitter and Facebook posts of salaried trolls; and in the curricula of schools, run by the RSS and its sister organisations, for poor children.

Muslims are declared to be multiplying at an alarming rate (expressed in the phrase 'Hum panch, hamaare pachees', or we five, our twenty-five) an outcome of Muslim men being allowed four wives, all of them reproducing prolifically. This is actually illogical and counter-factual, but can be read as reflecting the envy of the Hindu male, on whom the law has imposed monogamy, and is contrasted with the family planning slogan, 'Hum do, hamare do' (we two, our two) that Hindus presumably follow. Muslim men are said to be enticing Hindu girls into 'love jihad', deceitfully converting them to Islam. Muslim women need to be rescued from Muslim men, who are inclined to abandon them by uttering 'talaq' three times. They eat beef, thus being responsible for the killing of our holy mother, the cow. As neighbours, they are a nuisance because they regularly cook meat (never mind that the majority of Hindus eat meat) and once a year, during Bakr Id, they bring goats into society compounds and slaughter them in a cruel fashion. The construction of Muslims as the enemy is deliberate, and many of these pronouncements can be found in the old publications of the RSS going back to the1920s. They are aimed at uniting Hindus, whose everyday sense of identity is, in actuality, based on caste, linguistic and regional differences. The kind of 'unity in diversity' that is being propagated these days is based on a unity *against*. After 2014, this unity against has led to a new level of impunity for violence against Muslims.

Although the version of the Hindu religion being celebrated today is distinctly Brahmanical and patriarchal, women of all social groups have on occasion been active, even eager, participants in the violence against Muslims. This was most apparent during L.K. Advani's rath yatras in the 1990s, when trucks carrying facsimiles of Rama's chariot rode through northern states, demanding that a Rama temple be rebuilt on the site in Ayodhya where, it was claimed, the Mughal emperor, Babar, had razed such an edifice and erected a mosque, the Babri Masjid, in its place. Ayodhya was the mythological capital of Rama's kingdom, but the supporters of Hindutva claimed that the Rama temple had historically existed at the site of the Babri Masjid. Communal riots followed in many places in the wake of the rath yatra which culminated in the demolition of the Babri Masjid on December 6, 1992, by a mob armed with suitable tools and weapons, in full view of the police and the media, including international TV crews.

There were many women in the demolition squad of kar sewaks, or servants of action, some of whom had travelled long distances to reach the mosque. And there were also some prominent women from right-wing organisations, including fromthe RSS,who did the job of rabble-rousing. The fiery rhetoric of Sadhvi Rithambhara called on Hindu men to demonstrate their masculinity by avenging the insult to the god Rama, and there were many women, as well as men, who rose to the call. I remember the mother of a (non-Brahmin) anti-caste activist friend explaining to me, in strangely sensuous words, why she, in total opposition to her son's ideology, wanted to be a kar sewak: 'I want to roll on the ground and cover myself with the holy dust of Ayodhya.'

Reports from the ground in Gujarat during February-March 2002, also record the participation of women in the brutal acts of violence, arson, and the murder of Muslims. Many Dalits and Adivasis were also involved in the violence, an example of the success of the 'politics of othering' in achieving its goals.

Why do women buy into the overtly masculinist and misogynistic project of Hindutva? Why do they go to the extent of committing violence in its name? The feminist scholar, Paola Bacchetta,[1] has tried to answer this question by looking more closely at the RSS and its 'sister' organisation, the Rashtra Sevika Samiti.

Bacchetta does not think it is enough to attribute this to a kind of 'false consciousness' among women responding to such a masculinist call: that they were simply going along with the cause their men espoused, or with their caste group or their community. We have seen that the appeal by the RSS attracted not only upper castes, but a large number from the middle castes, the Bahujan and Other Backward Castes, or OBCs.[2] Bacchetta maintains that women who participate in these right-wing organisations, campaigns and violent attacks do so out of 'conviction, opportunism and active choice'.

Although Bacchetta does not say so, women in the Rashtra Sevika Samiti are usually encouraged to marry, as unmarried women might endanger the self-discipline of male Sangh activists, for whom celibacy is the ideal. The life of a married woman, catering to the needs of her husband and children, is what is prescribed for women. Even the founder of the Rashtra Sevika Samiti, Laxmibai Kelkar, who became active in Sangh-related programmes as an unmarried young woman, eventually married Purushottam Kelkar, a widower with two children. Of course, we have some prominent Hindutva activists who are described as 'Sadhvis': Rithambhara, who was vocal in the run-up to the demolition of the Babri Masjid, and Pragya Thakur, who is an accused in the Malegaon blasts case of 2008, and is now a BJP MP; but the majority of women in the Samiti and those who take active part in riots, are married women. In the RSS discourse, however, as Bacchetta observes, Hindu women are rarely referred to as wives; they are always addressed, and mentioned, first, as 'sisters' of male Sangh activists, and, in general, as 'mothers'.

We have discussed elsewhere the representation of the Muslim male as the enemy, as sexual predator and terrorist; this narrative has many layers. Bacchetta presents material from several publications and policy documents of the RSS and analyses the nature of this continuing discourse, its methods and its objectives. She says:

> Where possible, the RSS uses Brahminical symbols and signifiers to render the discourse familiar to its upper-caste and, more recently, upwardly mobile lower-caste audience, to disguise its political nature, to lend it moral sanctity, and therefore legitimacy.... *The RSS ideologues are more concerned with evoking response than with facts* (emphasis mine). For this reason, and because the discourse is unclosed, constantly

evolving through time, it easily accommodates contradictory statements and images.

The Muslim woman is variously represented as a helpless being oppressed by Islamic norms and structures, forced to wear the veil, suffering under polygamy, hemmed in by Muslim personal law; as a reproductive body producing a burgeoning Muslim population; as an oversexed being desiring Hindu men who are, however, wedded to higher Hindu values; and, finally 'as objects of potential or realised communal and sexual appropriation'.

Hindutva and Christianity

Although Christians are a smaller minority, the fear syndrome with regard to them focuses on the apprehension that they are out to convert all Indians to Christianity. (This is a tall claim, when Christians form just 2.3 per cent of the population in India!) Missionaries working in health and education with Adivasis and Dalits are targetted, and churches are attacked, but the attitude towards Christians, promoted by Hindutva thought-shapers, is always ambivalent. Around Christmas in 2018, there were several reports of churches being attacked; the interference with other religions' festivals and celebrations is a particularly despicable aspect of Hindutva, but in 2019, WhatApp groups frequented by Hindutva bhakts suddenly erupted with messages conveying the Christmas spirit of love and peace towards all. I noticed the contrast with the previous year and, on the whole, welcomed it, but there was a disturbing angle to it, too. It seemed as if, in 2019, we could afford to join the Christians in their celebrations because the Muslims had been sufficiently identified and singled out as the enemy.

The fear, falsehood, and even the felicitation propagated by the Hindutva brigade are always political in their intent, but they also have a basis in the common-or-garden variety of notions among Hindus about other religions. In my childhood, I heard stories about Christians 'polluting' village wells by dropping bread into them. This is a peculiar characteristic of Hindutva's fear of the Other—contact with those outside the Hindu fold (as well as those within the fold who have been marked out) is polluting. It builds on certain beliefs, widely held by caste Hindus, that inform their daily practise; my mother's attitude towards pollution is an example of this. Christians also eat beef, but because of their smaller number they are not major players in the trade in animal products. It is principally their zeal to convert, and their existence as a polluting presence, that leads the Hindu to be wary of his Christian neighbour. Sikhs and Jains are part of the wider Hindu community, having grown out of it. Parsis are even smaller in number, located mainly in urban centres; they, too, run charitable institutions, but do not attempt to convert, so their good deeds can be admired and benefitted from without vilifying the community as a whole. As even many Brahmins among Hindus are eating more meat now, some pollution-related beliefs and restrictions based on them are conveniently relaxed, but a basic, deep-rooted revulsion for the polluting Other remains.

Women are also the polluting Other, during menstruation and after they have delivered a child. We can laugh at the swami who declared that menstruating women who cook will be reborn as she-dogs, but his views have led administrators of a girls' institute, run by his foundation, to force its wards to remove their underwear to prove that they are not menstruating.[3] An aggressive Hindutva solidifies existing subliminal Hindu anxiety into active harassment and assaults on women's privacy and bodily integrity. This anxiety, with its inconsistencies and internal contradictions, is sharpened by the polarising rhetoric of Hindutvavadis, but it needs to be reiterated that their rhetoric proceeds from the entrenched discriminations in Hinduism itself.

The need to rewrite history

The historian RomilaThapar, in her many scholarly writings,[4] reminds us that a Hindu 'community' as such did not exist in ancient India. Rather, there was a multiplicity of sects and cults, worshipping different local gods and interacting with each other. She talks of a Brahmanic tradition, confined to a small elite with an adherence to Vedic texts. Then there was Shramanism, which included 'a variety of Buddhist, Jaina, Ajivika and other sects' that 'denied the fundamentals of Brahmanism, such as Vedic sruti and smriti'. There was diversity among the Brahmana sects, too, some remaining orthodox while others accepted the beliefs of the Sakta and other sects that were 'in many ways antithetical to early Brahmanism'. She also holds that the essentials of Shaktism, with a central role for the mother goddess, can be traced back to Harappan times.

'Brahmanism,' says Thapar, 'came closest to having a subcontinental identity largely through its ritual functions and the use of a common language, Sanskrit,' which was, however, confined to a small elite. Brahmins, by the first millennium CE, gained political authority and were granted land which made them major landowners, but they had to negotiate with local sects in order to maintain their authority. Certain deities became important; pilgrimages linked different local sects. By the end of the first millennium, Brahmanism had established its dominance; Shramanism (including Buddhism, which largely vanished from India and spread eastwards in Asia) was displaced, or sects became castes and were absorbed into the caste identity.

In describing the Bhakti movements that came up in different parts of India by the early second millennium, Thapar maintains that they drew on the Puranic traditions of Saivism and Vaishnavism, but many of them opposed caste and claimed that every worshipper is equal in the eyes of the deity. Thapar's main claim is that there was no such thing as a Hindu community right up to the time of the Muslim conquests. What she calls Brahmanism did exist, as did a hierarchy of castes, but this structure was not uniformly rigid.

This analysis is consistent with Kancha Ilaiah's, when he says that he thinks of himself as belonging to an artisanal caste with its own gods, rituals related to work and the seasons, and the traditions of a working people, rather than as part of a pan-Indian, multi-caste Hinduism.[5] Although he does romanticise this aspect, he goes some way towards restoring the value and dignity of labour, so often denigrated, because those who labour are stratified by caste in Hindu society. The fact is that the gods worshipped, the festivals celebrated, and the rituals performed by people calling themselves Hindu have myriad sources in India's history (some of them commemorate conflicts between groups, so that a festival that is celebrated as the defeat of a rakshasa in the dominant Brahmanical narrative and practice may have a completely different significance for subordinated sections and castes); but there is, and has been, a Brahmanical homogenisation in the dominant culture and media that is only now being challenged.

The nine-day Navratris, culminating in Dussehra, are a good example. A strange kind of homogenisation of the festival has taken place in Maharashtra in recent years. Navratri used to be a private family observance. In my family, and among CKPs more generally, a three- (or sometimes four-) generation kinship group would come together to honour the goddess, who is called Ambabai among us, and Mahadevi elsewhere in Maharashtra. Of late, however, a kind of leaking of the private into the public, a transformation of private observance into public spectacle has taken place. The goddess is installed in public, much like Ganesha during the Ganapati festival, that has been a public event since Bal Gangadhar Tilak inaugurated the public Ganeshotsav or Ganesha festival as a celebration of Hindu religious culture in the face of British rule. Often, especially in smaller towns, the Ganapati pandals are not dismantled and are used for the goddess, who arrives after a little more than a fortnight. This is the new Hinduism, where private worship is brought into the public and commercialised.

So, writing today about my relation to Hinduism, I observe these changes in religious practice with mixed feelings. Not being a believer myself, I used to regard the women and young girls around me in Aurangabad—who fasted for nine days with a proper meal only at night (sometimes only fruit), who walked barefoot every morning to the temple of the devi—with a certain respect for their devotion. This austere regime that they imposed on themselves and observed with utmost strictness to honour the matriarchal goddess, their celebration of the earth's fertility, seemed to my feminist eye to be somewhat liberating, certainly when compared to the austerities undertaken under a patriarchal sun or moon, to gain, retain, and honour a good husband. I also observed a camaraderie among the girls voluntarily undertaking this fast together; weekly or twice-monthly fasts are usually an individual affair.

In Marathi, and other Indian languages too, people often say, 'Today is my Tuesday', meaning, today is Tuesday, the day *I* keep a fast. These fasts seem to me to be a part of the culture of eating in Hindu homes, when the adult women of the house, and sometimes even young girls, eat only after the men have satisfied their appetites. Shared family meals are not a part of Hindu culture. On the other hand, in

Christian homes, and many Muslim ones, family meals are treasured as an occasion for all to come together; and fasts are also observed in common. The everyday practices of Hinduism, by contrast, are based on the division into castes, and on the subjugated and subordinate status of women. This is sometimes celebrated as one aspect of the 'pluralism' of Hindu religious practice: one can choose which god to worship, and on which day to fast.

Religion is also an occasion for social mingling, but among Hindus this, too, is inflected by caste. Pilgrimages are an excuse for travel; there are now many commercial packages for devotional travel, catering to specific food preferences, and specific castes. I have no real problem with this mixing of the traditional and modern, especially if it provides some flexibility in the strict regulation of young women's mobility; but, more and more, it is the most patriarchal rituals, like the *karva chauth*, that are glorified as prime examples of 'Indian culture'. This is a rigorous fast undertaken by women (formerly only in north India) in the month of Kartik, around September-October, which celebrates the patriarchal marriage as a relationship in which the wife must make sacrifices for the husband's good health and long life. Hindutva's endeavour to portray Hinduism as a pan-Indian religion inevitably reinforces caste and patriarchy. The market and commercial media enthusiastically take up this cause as their patriotic duty, and bombard us with images of decked-up women (and, these days, decked-up men), obviously and typically upper-caste in appearance, in suitably plush settings, with all the visual markers of Hindu (read Brahmin) religious devotion.

Leaders of the independence movement, the Indian National Congress, and progressive historians also constructed their own simplifications. They underlined the coexistence and symbiosis of Hindus and Muslims over centuries, and directed the struggle for independence against the tyranny and cruelties of British rule. The problem with this interpretation is that it downplays the violence and tyranny of Muslim rulers, who behaved like any rulers in mediaeval times. Conquest of territory and plunder of wealth were their main objectives, not conversion to Islam. Temples were looted, yes, but Hindu rulers, too, looted and destroyed Buddhist viharas in earlier times.

What makes the arguments and the partisanship even more confusing is the fact that lower-caste Hindu reformers like Jotirao Phule saw British rule as enabling the entry of Untouchables and Shudras into education, something they had been denied in caste society. (One should mention here that Phule had a clear understanding of how gender inequality and caste hierarchy worked in tandem. Along with Shudra-Atishudra to denote the oppressed sections of society, he uses the term Sarvastree-purush, or all women and men, when speaking of humankind.)[6] Some modern upper-caste liberals and leftists criticise Phule for his attempts to negotiate with the British on the issue of education, although it is clear from his writings that he had no illusions about the imperialist interests of the British regime. Similar criticism was directed at Ambedkar when he began negotiating with the British on separate political representation for Untouchables. Hindu society *is* a caste society, and that is why the construction of the Muslim as the main enemy inevitably means glossing over the reality of caste, in order to project a 'unified' Hinduism. At the same time, the Hindu order *is* a Brahmanical order; to preserve it the caste system and its hierarchy must be kept intact.

Gandhi's attempt to counter this became somewhat complicated; he was opposed to anti-Muslim communalism, but wanted the Hindu community to remain intact: with the caste system, but without untouchability. Ambedkar, on the other hand, made it clear in *Annihilation of Caste* that untouchability could not be removed as long as caste remained. Both leaders recognised the importance of religion in India, and both were dedicated to the principle of building India as a secular nation. Gandhi's strategy was to call on Hindus (read upper-caste Hindus) to undergo a kind of self-purification, voluntarily performing tasks considered to be polluting and relegated to the Dalits, without disturbing the caste-based division of labour. Ambedkar chose the path of conversion to Buddhism and called on his fellow Dalits to do so, but died soon after. Both leaders were deeply pained by Hindu-Muslim violence in the early 20th century, and both ultimately reconciled themselves to the inevitability of Partition.

I personally have not agonised over the Gandhi vs. Ambedkar debate and its many readings by those who try to reconcile the two. My affinity is definitely with Ambedkar. Both Gandhi and Ambedkar tried to balance their deeply-held convictions with the realities of politics and of society. I have lived too long myself now to expect consistency, even from our elder statesmen; but I do recognise and admire integrity, a much more complex quality.

My encounter with the composite culture of Aurangabad

My experience of Islam and Muslim culture comes from over thirty years spent in Aurangabad, from 1979 onwards. This city now has about one million inhabitants and is the capital of Marathwada, the Marathi-speaking part of the erstwhile state of Hyderabad. It still has a large Muslim population (although it has declined from about 40 per cent in 1950 to 30 per cent currently), and also a higher percentage of Dalits than the average for Maharashtra. Ambedkar chose Aurangabad as the location for several colleges, and was granted an area of 54 acres by the Nizam of Hyderabad for building educational institutions.

Mediaeval Islamic architecture is still an essential element of the city's landscape. The old Aurangabad was a gated town, and the names of the gates—Kaala Darwaza, Dilli Gate, Mohammed Darwaza, Roshan Gate, Makai Gate—evoke memories of my life there. We lived in the Marathwada University (later Dr. Babasaheb Ambedkar Marathwada University) campus for many years, and some of the most important monuments of the city were within walking distance. Bibi-ka-Maqbara, the monument Aurangzeb built around his wife's tomb, a copy of the Taj Mahal but without the marble and the splendour, is still dear to denizens of Aurangabad. The elaborate network of aquifers and canals that bring water to Aurangabad, constructed in the reign of Malik Ambar in the 17th century, are still functional, but the famous Paan Chakki, or water mill, no longer grinds wheat flour. Many of the old buildings have been converted into government offices. The whole city has a Muslim cultural ethos that visually impacts the eye. There are, of course, temples as well, some of them in the old city centre, and I recall at least three new temples that came up while we lived there, a Shiva temple and two dedicated to Ganesh; all of them large and elaborate, announcing their presence in visually high decibels.

Aurangabad was home to a number of well-known Urdu poets writing in Dakkhani Urdu, typical of the region. I came to know some of them quite well, as my husband, Tulsi Parab, translated some of their poems into Marathi.

After the communal riots of 1988, which followed the Shiv Sena's expansion from Bombay into rural Maharashtra, I witnessed a change in the city's social geography. Muslim families, among them some of our friends, sold their houses in hitherto mixed areas and moved to Muslim-dominated colonies. Some Hindus also moved house. Before our eyes the city became segregated along religious lines: there are now Muslim areas, Hindu areas, and Dalit areas. Even in what is called New Aurangabad, developed after 1990 by the City Industrial Development Corporation or CIDCO, Muslims are usually kept out of housing societies dominated by Hindus. With middle-class families belonging to the Scheduled Castes, the boycott is not explicit, but most Dalits are to be found living with neighbours from their own caste groups.

Over the years, the Muslim sections of the city have been sorely neglected by the municipal corporation. This is evidenced by the poor condition of the roads, infrequent visits by garbage-collecting trucks, and a generally run-down state. Hindus usually keep away. To some extent, this discrimination has been masked in recent years by the overall neglect of basic urban services everywhere, which has affected garbage disposal, the provision of clean water and the condition of roads in the city as a whole.

While recent attacks on Muslims in India—especially after the general elections of 2014, and greatly stepped up after Narendra Modi's and the BJP re-election in 2019—are horrifying, my years in Aurangabad gave me a first-hand encounter with how majoritarian Hindu India treats its Muslims on a daily basis. I saw a pattern here that is widely applicable to other places in the country. First, a history of Hindu-Muslim violence, with tacit state support, which is glossed over and subjected to the violence of silent suppression. Then, occasional riots that exacerbate animosity and force the minority community into a defensive solidarity among themselves. This prepares the ground for some young men (and possibly women) to be attracted to a more 'fundamentalist' Islam, which in turn, does not go unnoticed and creates a generalised suspicion. This, then, often informs routine police activity against Muslim youth, amounting to daily harassment, and more.

Aurangabad is not, on the whole, a city hostile to its women. When I first started working as lecturer in the university, Muslim women students, most of them from well-off urban backgrounds, would come to the department in their burkhas but discard them in class. Later, the sight of women in buses and on mopeds with long scarves covering their heads and sheltering their faces—from harsh sunlight, dust, and the male gaze?—became common. These were mainly Hindu women. As Aurangabad is an educational hub with many colleges, there are plenty of young women in public spaces. More recently, we frequently saw young Muslim women covered in full hijab, riding two-wheelers. All these women, across religion and generation, making compromises with tradition and attaining a modicum of freedom, are typical examples of the changes taking place in smaller towns in India.

Aurangabad, being near the international tourism sites of Ajanta and Ellora, has its own Buddhist caves, right behind the university, and has become a site of Dalit pilgrimage: hundreds of neo-Buddhist devotees visit every Buddha Purnima (the full moon night in the month of May) and Dussehra, the day on which Dr Babasaheb Ambedkar converted to Buddhism in 1956. Dalits have also gathered at the university gate on January 14, every year, since 1994, when Marathwada University was renamed Dr. Babasaheb Ambedkar Marathwada University, fulfilling a long-standing demand by them.

On the whole, the city is friendly to these pilgrims, unlike Mumbai, where gatherings of Dalits at Chaitya Bhoomi in Shivaji Park—where Ambedkar was cremated after his death on December 6, 1956—are generally considered a nuisance and a disturbance to the (Hindu) social order. Similarly, Aurangabad is sanguine about the big gatherings of Muslims at the Eidgaah Maidan on the occasion of Eid though, of late, middle class Hindus have been grumbling about such manifestations of Muslim cultural presence in the city. The intricately woven fabric of a composite culture is fraying, and it may be that attempts will be made to tear it apart in the near future.

Hindutva and Buddhism: politics of the calendar

For Hindutva, the Muslim is the Other without, while the Dalit, placed outside and below the chaturvarna hierarchy, is the 'Other' within. This has not been altered by Dalit conversion to Buddhism. The othering is reiterated on a daily basis, through discrimination in educational institutions and workplaces; through an ever-present threat of violence, made actual often enough to keep the threat alive; through the law and its mechanics of implementation; and finally, through cultural appropriation. While India's cultural diversity is vocally celebrated, there is, too often, a contempt for what 'others' hold sacred, their taboos, their symbols and icons. The most bizarre example of this is the encroachment of cultural space in the calendar. It took me some time to understand this.

When I heard that Buddha Purnima fell on May 18 in 2019, I suddenly woke up to some strange realisations. I remembered that Pokhran I, India's first nuclear test, took place on May 18, 1974, 45 years earlier—that was when I returned permanently to India, from England. The coded message from nuclear technologists to the government, indicating successful completion of the operation was: 'The Buddha is smiling'. I didn't realise then, and not until an odd suspicion led me to look it up on the Internet, that it was Buddha Purnima, occurring on May 18, as it did in 2019. The next date I looked up was that of Pokhran II, which was May 11, 1998 (five explosions spread over three days, May 11–13). Surprise, surprise, Buddha Purnima fell on May 11 in 1998. The second choice of date was clearly deliberate. The first time, I imagine, the scenario may have been as follows: May 18 is chosen for the nuclear test, known only to a small group of scientists and Indira Gandhi's office. Just then one of the former, a physicist with sandalwood paste smeared on his forehead, says, 'Oh, that's Buddha Jayanti. Why don't we use Buddha in our completion message?' The second time, however, with the BJP government under Atal Behari Vajpeyi, the choice was undoubtedly deliberate. After all, five and a half years earlier, the day of Dr Ambedkar's death or Mahaparinirvan, had been chosen for the demolition of Babri Masjid, December 6, 1992.

Another example of a Hindu-centric play with dates and calendars: Marathwada University was renamed Dr. Babasaheb Ambedkar Marathwada University on January 14, 1994. This was Makar Sankranti, the winter solstice, the only Hindu festival that follows a solar calendar. So we in Aurangabad were assured of a holiday, which we didn't have earlier for this festival. The 'Jai Bhimwallahs' could celebrate 'their' renaming, while the Hindus enjoyed their *haldi-kunkus* and kite-flying with a holiday...

More than sixty years ago, Babasaheb Ambedkar's conversion to Buddhism was emulated by millions of Dalits, first from Maharashtra and then from other states; initially the Mahars, followed by other 'untouchable' castes. When Ambedkar died soon after, this embrace of Buddhism became not just an assertion of identity for Dalits, but an avowal of faith in Ambedkar's path to social change; in a reasoned rebuttal of Hinduism's dogmas and rituals; and in a self-affirming rejection of caste discrimination. But Hindu society ever-so-subtly, and often blatantly, scorned and derided the religious celebrations of the new faith. That is where the desecration of Buddha Purnima comes from. Buddhism is seen, at once, as part of Hinduism, and as the creed of a socially marginalised community trying to assert a new identity of self-respect. That assertion is bitterly resented by the privileged few in our caste society.

This is an account of changes that have taken place from a more-or-less secular political climate to one clouded over by covert Hindutva intentions, on any available occasion. We need a radar of socially-grounded rationality to penetrate these clouds. Just as Muslims (minorities) on the one hand are treated differently from Scheduled Castes and Scheduled

Tribes in the Indian Constitution, so the 'othering' of these social groups works differently in Hindu-majority society. Violence against Muslims requires, or used to require, an excuse: desecration of a Hindu temple, or desecration of a mosque, inviting retaliation. In the last few years, however, even this excuse has become redundant; now the violence against Muslims is egregious and sanctioned.

Violence against Dalits, on the other hand, is woven into the very fabric of caste society, and has never needed external provocation. The *Manusmriti* spells it out: different punishments for Brahmins and Shudras, for the same crime. The murder of a Shudra, or a Dalit, by a Savarna is not a crime. The sexual availability of Dalit women to upper-caste men is taken for granted. Rape of a Dalit woman is not considered rape in India, any more than marital rape is.

While I have tried to highlight how modern Hindu society's othering of Muslims and Dalits has different bases, the different practices of othering work jointly to constitute the unique character of Hindu identity. This identity is based fundamentally on exclusion, both within and outside the community. The exclusion reiterates the superiority of the Brahmin male and the upper-caste male, in every instance: social death of the widow and her exclusion from auspicious ceremonies; the exclusion of the (polluting) menstruating girl from the temple and the hearth; the exclusion of women of reproductive age and of Dalits from the temple.

This is why my identity is not that of a Hindu woman.

References

[1] Paola Bacchetta, *Gender in the Hindu Nation: RSS Women as Ideologues* (New Delhi: Women Unlimited), 2004. I also profited from discussions with Supriya Gaikwad, whose M.Phil dissertation examines the Rashtra Sevika Samiti in Maharashtra.

[2] In her (Marathi) book, *Tichi Bhakri Koni Chorli?* (Who Stole her Bhakri?), journalist-researcher Sandhya Nare-Pawar has, on the basis of extensive interviews and recordings, shown how married and unmarried women among the OBCs are heavily influenced by the preaching of self-styled gurus and godmen, whose discourses inevitably reinforce caste norms and a misogynist, not to mention anti-Muslim, set of values.

[3] Swami Krushnaswarup Dasji, who made these remarks, is associated with the Swaminarayan Trust which runs a college in Bhuj; its principal and female staff allegedly forced more than 60 girls to remove their undergarments to check if they were menstruating (Press Trust of India, February 18, 2020).

[4] Romila Thapar, *History and Beyond* (New Delhi: Oxford University Press), 2004, makes most of the arguments mentioned here.

[5] Kancha Ilaiah Shepherd, *Post-Hindu India* (New Delhi: Sage), 2004.

[6] G.P. Deshpande (tr.), *Selected Writings of Jotirao Phule,* op.cit.

4 Caste and Anti-Caste

Part 1: The many faces of caste: privilege and its awareness

In the first three chapters I wrote about how caste and patriarchy lie at the core of the Hindu social structure, and that caste is ubiquitous in Indian society. Earlier, when anyone talked about caste, they were castigated for being 'casteist'; even Ambedkar had to face this accusation. This is changing, mainly because an assertion by Dalits over the past few decades has gradually made it acceptable to talk about how caste affects us all, about the invisible privileges that the upper castes enjoy. In the first part of this chapter I will speak about my own experience of caste as an upper-caste woman who spent her childhood abroad and has lived in India since young adulthood. The second part will discuss my participation in the anti-caste movement, and what I have learned about resistance to the caste system.

From 1976 to 1979 I lived in Sangamner, a tehsil[1] town in Ahmednagar district of Maharashtra, dominated by a sugar factory, with a pretty decent mofussil[2] college where I taught, and a robust history of local grassroots politics. My move to this rural place, almost straight from Cambridge, of course clothed me in a certain kind of privilege. I was allotted a flat in the faculty quarters on the university campus by the principal, MV Kaundinya, a liberal Brahmin who had collected funds to set up the college, on a co-operative basis, by going door-to-door. This was in consonance with the history of co-operative movements in western Maharashtra.

Among my neighbours was Rao Saheb Kasbe, who later became one of the leading intellectuals of Maharashtra, and was at the time engaged in writing a book on Golwalkar and the RSS.[3] His maternal uncle, Daya Pawar, had recently published one of the first Dalit autobiographies in Marathi, *Baluta*.[4] In fact, many of my colleagues in the college later became well known in their own fields: a novelist, a scholar of folk literature, a literary critic and a linguist. This was my introduction to the world of intellectual discourse in Marathi, at a time when my knowledge of Marathi was still rather limited. I was really lucky in this. I had applied for this job at random, wanting to get away from Pune, where I had experienced a kind of social claustrophobia.

I engaged with people in Sangamner via my own intellectual mission as a young Marxist. I also tried to connect with working-class organisations and struggles in this small town, but I was still not sensitive to the caste contradictions in it. My decision to leave Pune for a rural college was somewhat wild, though fortunately it turned out to be much better than I could have hoped for or anticipated. Among other pluses, it was where I met and married Tulsi Parab, son of a textile mill worker, belonging to the caste of peasants or Kunbis, whose family came from the coastal Konkan region, but who was very much a metropolitan being himself, a citizen and poet of Mumbai.

From 1979 to 2013, Tulsi and I lived in Aurangabad, the main city in Marathwada, a backward region of Maharashtra, and it was there that I really began to learn about the workings of caste in modern India.

As most of my childhood was spent in Singapore, it took me some time to become aware of caste at all. Of course, it had a sizeable Indian community, most of whom were Tamil-speaking descendants of labourers brought over by the British. There was a *class* divide between them and people like 'us'. In my parents' social circle, there were Indians from all over the country, from different states, distinguished from each other by the language they spoke at home and their region-specific culture. It was, therefore, our regional origin that became the primary marker of identity, together with class; we were a 'cosmopolitan' set of people who belonged to the upper middle-class, who in turn were, of course, mainly Hindu and upper-caste.

There were few occasions when caste was a topic of conversation at home. Sometimes there would be a reference to our CKP food habits. Our small-in-number non-Brahmin community, Kayasths by name but confined to Maharashtra, mostly urban-based and affluent, takes pride in being connoisseurs with regard to food (and drink. Even the women drink quite openly–including women of my mother's generation—something which elicited ridicule from other caste groups.) If any other caste was mentioned, it was usually Brahmins, by which my parents meant Maharashtrian Brahmins, especially the Konkanastha Brahmins, dominant in Pune and other cities of western Maharashtra and the coastal regions. It was only later, after living in caste society in India for some time, that I understood the subtle aura of entitlement that some of our Brahmin guests carried, which my parents referred to as 'stinginess'. Entertaining Brahmins, feeding them, is, after all, something that brings punya, or credit, in terms of virtue recognised by the divine.

We did not come into contact with other caste groups; the difference between us and the working-class Tamils we encountered was, as I have said, perceived more as a difference of class, language and culture, than of caste, per se. I do remember that, on one occasion, my mother had to prepare a meal for a visiting senior bank official, a Tam-Brahm who refused to eat hotel food. No onions, no garlic, etc. She called the wife of one of my father's junior Tamil colleagues for recipes for sambar and chutney, and was so successful that she was asked to cook for this official every time he visited Singapore! I recall concluding from this incident that 'all South Indians are strictly vegetarian'—I had never socially 'met' a non-vegetarian from South India. We were, after all, living outside India at a time when South Asian diasporas were not so widely dispersed, or so numerous, as to have carried the baggage of caste wholesale into the societies they emigrated to.

My childhood years, and our location in a rapidly changing Singapore, gave me a specific kind of insight that made me see things differently from my upper-caste peers after I returned to live in India.

My parents' liberal ideas were remarkably consistent, though they had all the limitations that upper-caste liberalism has: they came from a place of privilege, of having servants at home as well as, in my father's case, subordinates in the office. I had never seen them treat subordinates or servants with contempt or even condescension. There are two instances of behaviour, very different from my family's norm, that stand out in my memory. During a family visit to India when I was eight years old, we were staying with a cousin who had a daughter my own age. They had a live-in servant who came from Bihar, a man about forty years old, but I don't, to this day, know which caste he belonged to. His demeanour made me cringe: the obsequiousness of his gestures and his speech; his ever-readiness to be useful to those he deemed his superiors; the way that the children of the house behaved with him, not rudely as such, but accepting his devotion as the norm; all these were new to me and made me extremely uncomfortable though I did not, of course, label them as feudal then—I was only a child.

The second incident took place in Singapore, around the same time. A new entrant to our social circle was the family of a man who held a highly-paid job in something to do with finance; my father often mentioned how 'brilliant' he was. They lived in a huge bungalow, much larger than ours, with sprawling grounds. As we were getting ready to go home one day (for some reason he was arranging for us to be dropped in his car) the driver was a bit late in responding to his summons. When he did eventually turn up, our host asked him harshly in Malay, 'What took you so long? We are all waiting for you.' The driver answered, using a common Malay euphemism for urination, 'I had gone to throw away water.' His employer, obviously ignorant of Malay, was even more infuriated by this answer. 'What do you mean? Are you laughing at me?' The whole confrontation played out in front of both families, including the children, and I felt, first, an acute embarrassment, followed by a sense of injustice on the driver's behalf.

Looking back, I can read other social meanings into this incident. Our host, unlike most in my parents' social circle, belonged to an artisan caste. He seemed confident in social gatherings because of his success in his career; the incident recounted above was the only time I saw him lose his cool. But his wife was clearly a misfit. I did not at the time understand that some of this might be related to caste, how it is like an amorphous living form that changes shape and adapts to different settings and situations.

The kind of social discomfort and awkwardness suffered by the first generation of a caste that gains entry into occupations previously monopolised by higher castes, is palpable. Economic or professional success does not necessarily bring social acceptability to someone from a lower caste. Ambedkar's reminder that caste is a system of 'graded inequality' is pertinent to this example. The member of a middle caste, while he has ambitions of upward social mobility, is often uncomfortable in his relationship to those he considers to be below him, as well as with those whom he resents for being above him in the social hierarchy.

The 1960s, of which I am speaking, represented a period when independent India was entering its teenage years. We had a Constitution that outlawed untouchability. We had made provision for affirmative action in favour of the most discriminated castes and tribal groups, through reserved seats in legislative bodies, government jobs and education. But it would be many decades before the latter two yielded results in the form of greater numbers of Dalits in government service or in higher education, or among the middle class. In politics, representatives elected to seats reserved for Scheduled Castes and Tribes were not automatically better advocates of their communities' interest. This was what Ambedkar had feared when he made the case for separate electorates, rather than reserved seats; he believed that only those persons would get elected who had compromised with upper-caste voters. Still, many of us thought that it was somewhat obscene to talk about caste; paying attention to it would only perpetuate it. Caste was something practised by the 'uneducated', living in villages, not by the citizens of modern India.

Ignoring caste does not eliminate it; it just pushes it under the carpet. Only those who enjoy caste privilege can afford to ignore it. The CKP caste has a history of co-operation with the movement against untouchability. You will often hear declarations from members of this elite that they are not even aware of caste, that they don't practise caste, and by implication, that those who talk about caste are the ones perpetuating it. Our family was a part of this elite.

Every caste in the hierarchy has its own experience of caste, but it is so much a part of everyday life that it is internalised. Gopal Guru and Sundar Sarukkai have[5] written about how, in India, caste is seen as 'natural' rather than 'social', and its pervasive influence is located in the everyday. The sociologist, Suryakant Waghmore,[6] makes a similar point about caste being practised in 'polite' society. Caste also pertains to the intimate areas of one's life: those castes placed lower in the hierarchy have proverbs and sayings that talk about the ordinary, everyday functioning of caste, with an ironical humour that pokes fun at how the 'upper' castes think their values are superior.[7] But the irony of the caste system is that the 'middle' castes—which include those near the top *or* the bottom of the hierarchy—resent the humiliation or discrimination, the subtle or not-so-subtle exclusion they experience in everyday life at the hands of those who consider themselves superior, caste-wise. But they don't talk about it, especially those near the top, compensating by treating those lower in the hierarchy in the same way.

The CKP caste is confined to Maharashtra, is financially well-placed, educated and largely urban. Traditionally, CKPs think of themselves as Kshatriyas, although this has been disputed by Brahmins in the past.[8] Where the Kshatriyas *are* associated with kingly power and military prowess, and with dominant castes like the Marathas in Maharashtra or the Jats or Rajputs in north India, the connection of CKPs with the machinery of power has been as scribes, record-keepers and, in modern times, bureaucrats.

What is interesting is that there were a number of CKPs who supported anti-caste struggles, especially in the first half of the twentieth century, when Ambedkar was still alive. Even before Ambedkar took up the leadership of the anti-caste movement, there were those among the CKPs who supported the Dalits in their resistance against untouchability. In R.B. More's autobiography (published in English as *Memoirs of a Dalit Communist: The Many Worlds of R.B. More*)[9] is an account of how the young More, having done very well in the scholarship examination despite attending a village primary school, is nevertheless denied a seat in the high school at Mahad. The school premises are owned by a Brahmin who says he will close the school if an Untouchable is admitted. Hearing this, Ramchandra 'Bhikoba' Dhodapkar, a prominent CKP landowner, called the boy to his home, dictated some matter which he asked him to write on a postcard and send to a local newspaper's office. The news about the denial of admission to an Untouchable boy was published, and the next day the young boy was admitted.

Dhodapkar's grandson, K.S. or 'Prabodhankar' Thakre, was a well-known satirical writer and relentless critic of Brahmanical Hinduism. I quote from his essay, *The Religion of Temples and the Temples of Religion*,[10] to illustrate:

> The *Manusmriti*, the *Puranas*, and the temples form the threefold noose that the Brahminical priestly regime has

> hung around the neck of Hindu society in order to sustain the ritualistic domination of its caste, based on its supposed virtues. The moment someone attacks this core, all reformist and deformist Brahmins hiss like snakes in chorus, surprising many of our dim-witted intellectuals and gullible non-Brahmins even today (*translation mine*).

Surendranath Govind Tipnis was chairman of the Mahad Municipal Council at the time of the Mahad satyagraha in 1927, when Ambedkar led a movement to assert the right of Dalits to the water of the Chavdar reservoir in Mahad,[11] and many CKPs were office-bearers in institutions established by Ambedkar, such as the Siddharth College in Mumbai and Milind College in Aurangabad.[12]

I have never really identified with the CKP caste, but even when I was researching my translation of the R.B. More-Satyendra More text, questions persisted: why did a significant number of people from this caste join in the struggle against untouchability and caste? And why was this association discontinued later? I could find no traces of it from the mid-1970s onward. Some hints can be found in Ambedkar's writings. In *Who Were the Shudras?*[13] he examines the ancient roots of Brahmin control over how social groups are to be classified in the four varnas, and the privileges they are allowed in ritualistic and secular life. He also demonstrates how this control persisted in modern times; for instance, in the controversy over who would perform the coronation of Chhatrapati Shivaji, and according to which rituals Brahmins have the final word but are willing to bend the rules in exchange for copious bribes. Later, in the 19th and early 20th centuries, the Kayasths of Bengal and Bihar aspired to the status of Kshatriya and brought their claims to the courts of the British administration; but they are regarded as Shudras.

This Brahmanical hegemony over the ascription of caste status would have been strongly resented. Among Ambedkar's active supporters in his prolonged and bitter fight against caste and untouchability, were some Brahmins and members of the middle castes, but also a significant number of CKPs, in view of their small number. Later, however, as they acquired upper middle-class status in the modern political economy, the experience of caste humiliation was forgotten or denied, and an alliance with a progressive anti-caste movement was no longer seen to be part of caste history to be claimed with pride. There is now a disingenuous self-identification as 'almost like Brahmins', and CKPs have more often than not been supporters of the BJP.

It is interesting that Prabodhankar Thakre's son, Bal Thakre, founded the Shiv Sena as a party representing the interests of the Marathi son of the soil, mainly in the metropolitan setting of Bombay. Bal Thakre had the blessings of his father, who had been in the forefront of the movement to form a state based on the linguistic identity of Maharashtrians, carved out of parts of the Bombay Presidency, the Central Provinces and the Nizam-ruled state of Hyderabad. Starting with opposing non Maharashtrian control over trade and industry, the Shiv Sena evolved into a militant Hindu party, and in 1992–1993 oversaw violent anti-Muslim riots following the demolition of the Babri Masjid. But the Shiv Sena's mass base has always consisted of the Bombay working class, the middle castes, later officially categorised as Other Backward Classes. The Shiv Sena under Uddhav Thakre, having been a long-term ally of the BJP, is now opposing the latter's divisive anti-Muslim politics.[14]

The story of this caste into which I was born is illustrative of how caste as a *system* flourishes under changed social, economic and political circumstances.

When I was a student at Cambridge in the 1970s and participated in left-wing discussions and activities, I was uncomfortably aware of the fact that not much was said in Marxist circles about racism, or of relations between Britain and her ex-colonies. Although there was the camaraderie of intense reading and debate, of the occasional campaign or demonstration, I always felt a little apart. I had a different social history, a different culture at home; furthermore, I was Indian but, again, different from other Indians because of never having lived in India. There were, undoubtedly, personal and family reasons for enhancing this feeling, but mainly it was my social and geographical background that made for scepticism and an outsider's view about causes that I supported, together with my left-wing friends.

But being, or rather becoming, a feminist in the 1970s was an exhilarating experience. Here our aspirations, our appetite for new theories, and the experience of being part of a social movement all came together. We quarrelled with our male friends, cracked jokes, wrote pamphlets, visited the homes of ordinary housewives in Cambridge to form 'consciousness-raising' groups. Most of us came from comfortable middle-class backgrounds, but there was also the British welfare state, which paid for my university education. My father could not have afforded to keep me on at Cambridge without the munificence of the British welfare state. When my parents returned to India in my second year, I moved to rooms where foreign students were lodged.

Let me look now at two dictionary definitions of caste:

Merriam-Webster:

1: One of the hereditary social classes in Hinduism that restrict the occupation of their members and their association with the members of other castes.

2a: A division of society based on differences of wealth, inherited rank or privilege, profession, occupation, or race.

b: The position conferred by caste; standing, prestige: art and religion have lost *caste*—F.L. Baumer.

3: A system of rigid social stratification characterised by hereditary status, *endogamy*, and social barriers sanctioned by custom, law, or religion.

I am not looking at the etymology of the word or at its historic usage, rather at the layers of connotation it has acquired in contemporary contexts. The first meaning *is* linked to Hindu society; other definitions recognise that a rigid stratification of society into groups separated by 'custom, law or religion' may exist elsewhere as well; but it is Hindu society in which the caste system influences people's behaviour in all kinds of situations. It is most evident with regard to marriage and to food habits, to inter-marriage and inter-dining, but also in monitoring entry into an occupational space. It is here that caste operates most rigidly, often with violence being used to punish transgressions. There is enough evidence from specific studies and data in the public domain to show that higher education institutions, private sector corporations, and the print and electronic media are virtually the monopolies of the upper castes.[15] The domain of caste extends beyond, however, to embrace culinary traditions, language, modes of dress, ways of celebrating festivals, favourite deities, codes of etiquette, purity and pollution rituals, and, of course, temple entry. If, in the matter of marriage and occupation, it is men, patriarchs and caste elders who have the final word, in many other areas, in the everyday performance of caste, it is women who uphold caste identity.

The phrase 'caste Hindu' refers to all those castes that are not outcastes, i.e., to non-Dalits. One can 'lose caste' by transgressing the boundaries set by the caste system. So, for example, we hear of *nhavis* (barbers) being boycotted because they may have shaved Dalits, or of a family being excommunicated because one of its members married a woman from a 'lower' caste. This is how the middle castes in the hierarchy are recruited as 'foot soldiers' to police the boundaries of caste. This is how the women of the family are entrusted with the maintenance of the patriarchal order. Caste and patriarchy work beautifully in tandem here; upper castes can thus put on a 'progressive' face, claiming that it is not they, but the middle castes, who are discriminating against Dalits by committing acts of caste violence or enforcing caste endogamy. Similarly, men who benefit greatly from the patriarchal family order can always say that it is the women who are most hostile to other women. Today, many of the most openly vociferous, and occasionally violent, defenders of Hindutva belong to the middle castes, the artisan castes, those whom Jotirao Phule referred to as Shudras. Many are women. Here, too, one is mindful of the fact that many of the violent excesses and offensive pronouncements of right-wing Hindutva supporters only echo, and exaggerate, the sanctioned and routinised everyday practises of the caste system. The graded inequality that Ambedkar spoke of is crucial to keeping the hierarchy intact. We may add that it is graded *and* gendered, and both are intrinsic to caste patriarchy and to Hindutva.

Bertrand Russell, in *Why I am not a Christian*, says that the two essential features of being a Christian are (*i*) belief in God and immortality; and (*ii*) a belief that Jesus Christ, at the very least, was the best and wisest of men. This is a broad and generously accommodating definition, but what I want to underline here is that it rests on *believing* an essential something. Hindus, on the other hand, differ among themselves about what they believe in. Identification as a Hindu requires a *performative act*: visiting a temple to ask for blessings before launching a big scientific project, for example, is a social declaration of being Hindu. Belief in science and even atheism are acceptable, once the daily self-identification has been done. For the Brahmin male scientists who dominate scientific establishments in our country, the sandalwood paste on the forehead and the sacred thread under the shirt are necessary. Women scientists may be entering this space in larger numbers now, but it will be a long while before its caste composition changes. The scientific laboratory in India is inevitably a Brahmin, male-dominated space, and palpably unscientific behaviour is key to keeping it so.

Declaration of one's Hindu-ness, through actions that simultaneously announce one's religion and one's caste, are par for the course. Scientists apart, others, in other spaces and other contexts, also find ways to declare their Hindu identity. From the Shiv Sena's 'Garv Se Kaho Ham Hindu Hain' (Say With Pride, We Are Hindu) when it shifted, in the late 1980s, from an anti-South Indian, anti-communist agenda to a more openly anti-Muslim one; to the recent Maratha Andolan evoking Chhatrapati Shivaji and the martial pride of the Marathas; the political as well as the everyday declaration of one's religion is also a declaration of one's caste. The Maratha Andolan has introduced a new practice of women and men tying red and saffron-coloured *pheta*s (turbans)on their heads in ceremonial Maratha style, while riding on powerful motorcycles. Women's presence on these masculine symbols of power is deceptive—the Andolan has no interest in addressing gender inequality; the women on motorbikes simply endorse the patriarchal order.

It used to be the women, at least in Maharashtra, who displayed a caste/religious/tribal identity through their dress, ornaments and facial embellishment. B.R. Ambedkar, during the satyagraha in Mahad in December 1927, recognised this. Addressing the women on that occasion he said:

> The way you wear your saris is a sign of your being untouchable, you must wipe out that sign. You must begin the practice of wearing your saris in the same fashion that upper caste women do, it will not cost you anything. In the same way, your habit of wearing heavy necklaces around your necks, and bracelets and bangles made of base metal up to the elbow, mark you out as being untouchable. There is no need for more than one necklace.[16]

It is important to differentiate between the visible sartorial assertions of identity by dominant communities, and cultural assertions by the dominated. Equating the two is also a kind of politics, a politics of trivialising resistance by the Dalits, the Bahujans, and the dominated. Two examples may illustrate my point: a recent post on Facebook from BBC Marathi had the title: 'How is Dalit youth strengthening its social status?'[17] with a headline photo of two young women wearing *phetas* similar to those sported by women and men of the Maratha Andolan, but in dark blue, the colour of the Republican Party of India. They were also wearing shiny dark blue sunglasses. This is the flashy, ostentatious face of young Dalit resistance, or rather the one that the BBC chooses to showcase. The post talks about how young Dalits, with rapidly growing literacy, are staking claim to certain displays of social status—a bridegroom riding to the wedding on a horse, or wearing expensive and fashionable clothes, and so on, all likely to provoke an angry reaction from the upper castes. The post's overall message is that Dalits have now acquired the minimum skills required to become consumers in the global marketplace; their cultural assertion, their show of resistance, can be understood as an imitation of caste Hindu culture by the half-educated. It thereby simultaneously alerts the reader to this Dalit transgression, and dismisses it by defanging it.

My second example relates to the report of a Bahujan cultural festival organised by students at the Tata Institute of Social Sciences (TISS), Mumbai, in 2018. Regular cultural festivals, they felt, tended to be taken over by students from an upper-caste background; but now Dalit-Bahujan students are making films, producing art work, staging musical performances, so the festival brought these together on campus, over a period of two days. It drew an enthusiastic response, and received appreciative comments in the local supplement of a leading English-language newspaper. Well and good. But I was struck by the headline of the story: 'TISS *offers* platform to Dalit-Bahujan students'.[18] The wording should have been, 'Dalit-Bahujan students organise annual cultural fest'; a university should not be *offering* a platform to its Dalit-Bahujan minority. The implicit, unspoken *assumption* here is that the university space belongs to 'mainstream' (read upper-caste) students, a clear reflection of what caste privilege implies. Even with reserved seats for Dalit (SC category) and Adivasi (ST category) students in higher education being in place since the 1950s, and for OBC students since the 1990s, it is only very recently that students from less-privileged social backgrounds have gained entry to India's premier institutions. They face many obstacles, ranging from lack of fluency in English to insensitivity and hostility, even contempt, from the faculty for 'reserved-category students'. The headline I have quoted reveals how the privileged assume that the space of higher education belongs to them. Caste as privilege: invisible, unspoken, unspeakable, but always present. Essentially a Brahmanical privilege, so that even when other castes appear to hold power, a Brahmin is required to say, anoint the Maratha king, Chhatrapati Shivaji, and can refuse to do so.

Resistance by the unprivileged takes many forms and shapes, occurs in diverse venues and social locations. Things are changing. The market plays a role, too: sociologist Suryakant Waghmore distinguishes between state-driven and demand-driven change. Referring to how films on anti-caste themes have recently done well at the box office, he says:

> As caste-progressivism sells more, such performative progressivism will need to be assessed based on the challenges it poses to Hindu politeness and Hindu cosmopolitanism. Exploring the subtlety of caste privilege and oppression across public and private life will have a more critical role than dramatic reformism in art and cinema.[19]

When my husband, Tulsi, and I moved to Aurangabad in 1979, we found ourselves in a milieu where caste discrimination was rampant, and caste was talked about openly, without embarrassment. This was somewhat shocking to both of us. To me, because I had been living in Sangamner, working in a college with strong progressive roots, with a principal who valued his faculty and was appreciative and supportive of a Dalit scholar like Rao Saheb Kasbe. I had left my mother's home in Pune, piqued, because my brother Sudhir often put me down, saying I knew nothing of Indian society. I felt vaguely alienated from the group of young radical students that surrounded him, all from comfortable, urban, educated, upper-caste families, who talked of a Mao-style peasant revolution in India. My own Marxist perspective held me back from thinking explicitly about caste, or, for that matter, from reading Ambedkar. Tulsi came from working-class Mumbai and was also influenced by the Marxism prevalent in radical, left-wing circles. The chawl in which he lived had families from all over Maharashtra belonging to different castes, but not a single Dalit family. Tulsi himself had been a supporter of the Dalit Panthers and both its founders, Namdeo Dhasal and Raja Dhale, were once his close friends; but of caste in non-metropolitan Maharashtra he knew nothing. He had been an activist among Adivasis in rural Maharashtra, it is true; but the oppression they suffered took the form of exploiting their labour. As they were considered to be outside caste society, they were not treated as untouchable.

We had trouble renting a place to stay. Brahmin and Jain landlords did not ask us our caste directly, but we were obviously an inter-caste couple: anyway, they rejected us when we said we were meat-eaters. One thing that struck me forcefully was that the colleges in the city affiliated to our university were categorised by caste (or, to use a term invented by Suraj Yengde, young author of *Caste Matters*,[20] castegorised).The government college apart, all the others could each be identified by the caste of their management bodies, and the majority of their students. Colleges founded by Dr Ambedkar still existed, but there was now a Brahmin college, a Maratha college, a Muslim college, one catering to nomadic tribes, and a women's college run by the Vaisya or trader caste. Colleges established at Ambedkar's initiative to bring higher education to a backward region now catered mainly to Dalit students from Marathwada and Vidarbha. In the course of our long sojourn in Aurangabad the number of colleges grew, and though reservations have seen a change in the social composition of undergraduate students, college managements remain casteist in their approach.

Part 2: Anti-caste resistance: experiences and observations

One year before we moved to Aurangabad, Sharad Pawar, then chief minister of Maharashtra, announced that his government would confer the name of Dr Babasaheb Ambedkar on Marathwada University. Pawar's motivations were twofold: one, to convince people of his 'progressive' politics; and two, to secure a Dalit vote bank for his party. But his proposed *namantar*, renaming, of the university, immediately became a contentious issue. Dalits welcomed it, although it had not been a major demand of theirs, but the upper caste elite, comprising Brahmins and traders (who had led the agitation to end the Nizam's rule) and the Marathas, who then held political power, opposed the renaming as damaging to the regional identity of Marathwada.[21] The local daily, *Marathwada*, over a period of months, whipped up emotions against it, as a result of which there were several violent attacks on Dalits in the villages. Over the subsequent decade and a half, the Dalits then took it up as a rallying cry, and the university was finally named Dr Babasaheb Ambedkar Marathwada University (retaining the regional title) on January 14, 1994.

At the time, my thinking was still that of a traditional Marxist, and Tulsi's that of a working-class man from a 'middle' caste whose literary rebellion against the Brahmanical cultural elite had not been envisaged in terms of caste. The Little Magazine Movement of the 1960s, of which he was a part, saw itself as modern, if not 'modernist', in defiance of the literary conventions of the time, whose custodians were inevitably the Brahmanical elite. It was spearheaded by young *men* (like Tulsi), mainly from metropolitan Bombay but also elsewhere, who were in touch with world trends in literature and film. A good many of them came from the 'backward castes', with the occasional Dalit like Namdeo Dhasal and Raja Dhale.

The university renaming demand did not make much sense to us, as it seemed to bring no material benefits to Dalits, nor did it originate from the Dalit movement. But the lynching of Dalits, and other forms of violence against Dalit men and women throughout the region, as well as a newspaper campaign opposing the renaming, kept the demand alive. Caste itself, as an issue, was not much in the news in the decade of the mid-Eighties to the mid-Nineties, nor was it discussed in left-liberal debates. The threat of neoliberalism and of rising Hindutva forces were the preoccupations of that time.

In Marathwada, the renaming issue smouldered on. Demonstrators courted jail, there were more lynchings in the villages, and anti-caste student politics in Aurangabad city got a boost. In 1986–87, I published two papers, in collaboration with others, related to caste in the political economy of Maharashtra. I was still struggling with a Marxist perspective that refused to place caste at the centre of Indian society and its transformation. The phenomenon of aggressive Hindu nationalism and the neoliberal regime in the global economy were pivotal in our analyses and in our resistance. The connections between the two were fairly clear. In 1995, rumours of Ganesha idols actually 'drinking' the milk offered to them 'went viral', to use an anachronistic term.[22] Some say this was an experiment by the publicists of right-wing forces to test how far a gullible Hindu public could be made to swallow any nonsense that was fed to them, but we did not then talk about how *both* Hindu religious fundamentalism and global capital in their aggressive new avatar would rely on, and exacerbate, the hierarchical social order of caste patriarchy.

From 1997 to 2000, I became socially active again in a real sense, for the first time after I left Sangamner. (In the intervening years I had been preoccupied with my children and tragic events in my natal family.) This time it was with a group of people younger than us, who followed the thinking of Sharad Patil, dissident member of the Communist Party of India (Marxist), who had developed his own brand of Marx-Phule-Ambedkar-ism. These activists did not come from privileged, upper-caste backgrounds, they belonged to various non-Brahmin castes and to different regions of Maharashtra. I learnt from them about the realities of caste in the daily life of the non-urban and urban non-elite. They were discovering Gramsci, talking about the importance of culture in the maintenance of caste; therefore, also, of the importance of culture in the anti-caste movement. They had energy and coherence as a group; and for some time our house was filled with the comings and goings of activists. But the group fell apart due to internal contradictions, together with some resentment against me as an upper-caste woman. Caste contradictions also affect those who are trying to overcome caste. For instance, the group encouraged inter-caste marriages and, indeed, there were some successful pairings of this kind; but it is not easy for an ideologically constituted organisation to counter the conservative social forces that interfere with, and place obstacles in the way of, such unions.

This was a moment in India's political history when the Left, and all those trying to bring about social transformation in the direction of equality, were somewhat confused and adrift. The withdrawal of the state from earlier commitments to social welfare and the entry of foreign-funded NGOs left people's organisations ineffective and weakened. The steady rise of Hindu fundamentalism after the demolition of Babri Masjid resulted in many of us feeling shocked and helpless. But the connection of communal polarisation and sharpening economic inequality with caste was still not being drawn with enough insight and complexity.

Combining a discussion of gender with caste was a little more promising. Both Phule and Ambedkar had already made the links and I started reading Phule and Ambedkar, and writing about caste and gender, in this period.

Between 1995 and 2015, Indian feminists began taking note of caste, and of issues faced by Dalit women. Gopal Guru's 1995 article, 'Dalit Women Talk Differently'[23] argued that the experiences of Dalit women, and their feminist consciousness, were different, and that 'mainstream' feminism had not taken sufficient cognisance of this difference. In response, Sharmila Rege wrote about the possibility of non-Dalit feminists adopting a Dalit feminist standpoint,[24] which opened the way to a number of works in which established upper-caste women scholars wrote about Dalit issues and presented the work of Dalit women writers in English translation.[25] In 1996, the Alochana Documentation and Research Centre on Women, of which I am a founder-trustee, organised a workshop in Pune in which a number of Dalit women activists, writers, journalists, and scholars were invited to present their perspective on the women's movement and on issues that concerned them.[26] This was an early attempt, when Dalit women had only just begun to organise separately and to articulate their position.

An important work from this period was the 2003 book, *Gendering Caste with a Feminist Lens*,[27] by the Brahmin feminist, Uma Chakravarti, which analyses how caste and gender work together; and that 'caste is *constituted* by gender'. She writes as an upper-caste Brahmin feminist, and addresses upper-caste readers who may be conscious of feminist issues, but not of caste. She points out how the rules of caste endogamy are internalised by upper-caste women, using the example of many such women protesting against the extension of reservation to OBCs, to illustrate her point. She argues that it is Brahmanical patriarchy, exercising control over its women in the interests of caste purity, that imposes restrictions on upper-caste women; but lower castes emulate these practices, and patriarchy controls women among them, too.

Things have moved on since then, and there is now more (but still not enough) open talk about upper-caste privilege. The battle for a more equitable division of household chores has never been fought between urban middle-class men and women because of the ubiquitous availability of domestic labour—mainly from Dalits and Muslims for menial work, and for kitchen chores and cooking from a range of middle and upper castes.

The point I wish to make is that it is not enough that Dalit and Bahujan feminists are now being given a hearing. Is Dalit feminism something that concerns only 'them' directly, and 'us' only through empathy? Or does what feminists from a Dalit-Bahujan social location are saying call for revisiting our understanding of feminism in India?

Seventy years after India adopted a secular Constitution, and almost a hundred years after Ambedkar publicly burnt the *Manusmriti,* caste is alive and well in daily practise and in the minds and hearts of many Hindus. Untouchability is still practised, and it has religious sanction. Hinduism is founded on caste hierarchy, which is perpetuated by caste endogamy. And so this religious norm of excluding all those we call the Other penetrates the most intimate corners of our lives, and erupts as violence against women and Dalits in the public sphere. Hinduism has the subjugation of women and Dalits at its core. Project Hindutva, building a Hindu nation based on an exclusionary imperative, is erected on this core, and in recent years has come to dominate our political life. Its overt target is Muslims, but its mission is to preserve the hierarchies of gender and caste, which are inherent in Hinduism.

Resistance to caste has also always been part of our history and culture, but for a long time it remained submerged in an upper-caste domination of modern media and education. As a woman born into an upper-caste Hindu family I have, over the years, witnessed both the persistence of caste and the resistance to it that is emerging in contemporary discourse, and in new cultural challenges and assertions of equality. I cannot pretend to shake off my upper-caste origins, but I unequivocally reject the Hinduism that perpetuates their relevance.

References

[1] A tehsil consists of an area of land within a city or town that serves as its headquarters, with possible additional towns, and usually a number of villages. Tehsils are subdivisions of districts which are the administrative units into which every state of the Indian Union is divided

[2] Mofussil is a word dating back to the colonial era, referring to provincial or rural regions of India

[3] Rao Saheb Kasbe, *Decoding the RSS: Its Tradition and Politics* (New Delhi: Leftword Books), 2019. Originally published in Marathi as *Zot* (1978).

[4] Daya Pawar, *Baluta* (Marathi) trans. Jerry Pinto (New Delhi: Speaking Tiger), 2015.

[5] Gopal Guru and Sundar Sarukkai, *Experience, Caste, and the Everyday Social* (New Delhi: Oxford University Press), 2019.

[6] Suryakant Waghmore: 'Why Anti-Caste Movies Are Making Money', www.newsclick.in, September 11, 2019.

[7] Sangita Thosar, *Creating a Text from Oral Tradition*, unpublished project report, Tata Institute of Social Sciences, Mumbai.

[8] Ambedekar, in his 1946 book, *Who Were the Shudras?* cites several instances of disputes between Brahmins and Kayasths over the varna categorisation of the latter.

[9] Satyendra More, *Memoirs of a Dalit Communist: The Many Worlds of R.B. More* (trans. Wandana Sonalkar, New Delhi: Leftword), 2019.

[10] K.S. Thakre, *Devlancha Dharma Aani Dharmachi Devle* (Marathi, 1919).

[11] Anand Teltumbde has given an account of the Mahad satyagraha in *MAHAD: The Making of the First Dalit Revolt* (New Delhi: Aakar Books), 2016.

[12] M.B. Chitnis was the first principal of Milind College in Aurangabad when it was founded by B.R. Ambedkar. Later he was registrar of Marathwada University; I met him after he retired. Dhananjay Keer, biographer of Ambedkar, mentions in his *Ambedkar: Life and Mission* (1971) that V.S. Patankar was principal, and K.V. Chitre was registrar of Siddharth College, Bombay, in the 1950s. All these are CKP surnames.

[13] See Note 8 above.

[14] This is a recurrent theme in the speeches of Uddhav Thackeray as chief minister of Maharashtra, speaking to people on the Covid-19 crisis. See, for example, 'Coronavirus | Uddhav Thackeray warns against spread of "communal virus"', *The Hindu,* April 4, 2019.

[15] The suicide of Rohit Vemula, Dalit student of Hyderabad Central University in 2016, and that of Payal Tadvi, an Adivasi resident doctor at Nair Hospital, Mumbai, in 2019 speak of the cruel discrimination still practised, and have elicited widespread outrage. See also Sukhadeo Thorat, S. Madheswaran, 'Graded Caste Inequality and Poverty: Evidence on Role of Economic Discrimination', *Journal of Social Inclusion Studies*, 2018.

[16] An account of Dr Ambedkar's address to the Dalit women taking part in the Mahad satyagraha is given in Urmila Pawar and Meenakshi Moon, *We Also Made History* (trans. Wandana Sonalkar, New Delhi: Zubaan), 2008.

[17] 'How is Dalit youth strengthening its social status?', BBC Marathi.

[18] 'TISS offers platform to Dalit-Bahujan students', report in *Mumbai Mirror*, December 23, 2018.

[19] See Note 6 above.

[20] Suraj Yengde, *Caste Matters* (Gurugram: Penguin Viking), 2019.

[21] The autobiography of the activist, Eknath Awad (1956–2015), published in English as *Strike a Blow to Change the World* (New Delhi: Speaking Tiger), 2019, gives a good account of the Namantar movement.

[22] See, for example, the BBC news report, 'The "milk miracle" that brought India to a standstill', December 14, 2016.

[23] Gopal Guru, 'Dalit Women Talk Differently', *Economic & Political Weekly*, October 14–21, 1995.

[24] Sharmila Rege, 'A Dalit Feminist Standpoint', *Seminar*, October 1998.

[25] The list is long. Several of Urmila Pawar's books have been translated into English, as have the works of Dalit feminists writing in Tamil. Sharmila Rege (ed.), *Writing Caste, Writing Gender* (New Delhi: Zubaan), 2006, has presented translated extracts from, and summaries of the writings of Dalit women. I will mention two of my own contributions: Wandana Sonalkar, 'An Agenda for Gender Politics', *Economic & Political Weekly*, January 2, 1999; and 'Towards a Feminism of Caste', long review article in *Himal South Asia*, January 2004. In both these, I argue that listening to Dalit voices is important for our own understanding of patriarchy in Indian society.

[26] Some of the participants in this seminar contributed articles to a book in Marathi published by Alochana, *Dalit Striyanchi*

Asmita: Aavishkar Aani Disha (1999) (Dalit Women's Identity: Manifestations and Directions).

[27] Uma Chakravarti, *Gendering Caste with a Feminist Lens* (Kolkata: Stree), 2003. Uma Chakravarti published a new edition in 2018, after a gap of fifteen crucial years, adding an appendix which chronicles incidents of violence against Dalit women in recent years, shows how the perpetrators act with impunity, and how the machinery of the state protects them.

5 The Violence of Hinduism & Hindutva

In this chapter I turn to the subject of how violence is endemic to Hinduism, and to the social edifice that it erects. Violence directed against women and the lower castes, far from being seen as a crime, is considered legitimate and justified, both in the *Manusmriti* and in other religious texts. There is also plenty of violence in Hindu mythology, and what is notable is how it has inspired some of the violence we see in different spheres of life today. I explore the relationship between the violence of Hindutva that is being sold to us now with the specific, historically entrenched, violence of this particular religion, and the cultural traditions it gives birth to. I will also discuss what this has meant for the functioning of the Indian state, and very tentatively attempt to understand its psychological implications.

While we were in Aurangabad and lived on campus, we once had a strange visitor. This would have been towards the end of the 1990s, before I initiated a women's studies centre with its prescribed 'outreach' activities. My visitor was a clerk in a government department, and he came with a mission. He had read, in the local papers, about a woman somewhere in Maharashtra whose husband had cut off her nose because he suspected her of infidelity; but he then found that such cases were not uncommon. He did a bit of enquiring around, and learnt that prosthetics for such victims (fitting them with an artificial nose) could be carried out at government hospitals at minimal cost. This would make the woman's life a little more bearable. He then located and contacted one such woman, escorted her to the government hospital in Pune at his own expense, and followed up her case after treatment, to help if needed. He repeated this exercise with several affected women. He was a simple man, and wanted nothing from me except to ask that I should send any women in need of such help to him. I actually accompanied him on one of his expeditions and found that his behaviour with the woman in question was matter-of-fact and straightforward. He just wanted to do his bit to right a wrong that, apparently, recurs quite frequently in our society.

The story of Surpanakha in the *Ramayana* tells of Rama cutting off the rakshasi Surpanakha's nose because she dared to lust after him and his brother, Lakshman. Of course, there are different versions of the *Ramayana*, some of which are sympathetic to Surpanakha, and most versions say she was a great beauty. We may ponder the psychology behind this violent act of disfigurement. Could it be that the lord himself was tempted? If not, then does such random cruelty, stemming from a desire to punish, make any more sense? Of course, it is important to remember that Surpanakha was Ravana's sister, who later abducted Rama's wife, Sita.

Do these 20th and 21st century men who cut off their wives' noses think of themselves as emulating Lord

Rama, the ideal of manhood in the Hindu pantheon? Are the perpetrators, mainly husbands, imbued with self-righteousness, disciplining their wayward wives? Surpanakha apart, Rama also violently punished his own wife, Sita—is trial by fire not an act of violence?—despite the fact that the legend praises Ravana for respecting Sita's chastity. Morality for Sita means obedience to her husband, or his brother, Lakshman, in Rama's absence. She is abducted because she crosses the lakshman rekha, the threshold which symbolises the boundaries drawn by men around women's freedom and sexuality. The trial by fire after she is rescued from Ravana is not a test of her faithfulness, but of Rama's 'honour', and even though she emerges unscathed, she is banished.

These are powerful symbols, and the *Ramayana* has a central place in the Hindu imagination. The sanction given for punishment by violent disfigurement also flows from the *Ramayana*. Nose-cutting and acid attacks are mutilating; rape compromises the woman's chastity, and through her the 'honour' of the man or men who should be protecting her. Women are seen as a temptation to men (especially Brahmin and Kshatriya, 'twice-born' men) who must harness their virility so that they can serve a higher purpose; women's beauty is a snare, their sexual purity and faithfulness a prize to be guarded. Women of the lower castes are a means to remind lower-caste men that they do not have the power to protect their women. Much of the violence in Hinduism is grounded in inequality, on the principle that women (and Shudras) are born to serve and obey, and that the service and obedience of Dalits, doing their designated work, places them even lower than Shudras.

The *Ramayana* remains the guide for modern Hindu morality. It describes the ideal man, the ideal king. It speaks of devotion between brothers, of sacrifice to fulfil another's promises, of filial duty, and a man's love for his wife. Some time after the *Ramayana* serial started airing on state-owned television, my brother Sudhir carried out a survey, asking men and women, mainly from working-class backgrounds, what the *Ramayana* meant to them. He found that, although the epic does not propagate a communal view of Hinduism, the then Congress government sponsored its broadcast in order to win over a Hindu vote-bank that was being wooed by the Bharatiya Janata Party.[1]

When the other great Hindu epic, the *Mahabharata*, began airing on national television soon after, in October 1988, my younger son was three months old, and I was on extended leave in Pune, staying at my mother's place. Sudhir felt that for this story of a fratricidal war to be entering people's homes via television was an ominous portent. I remember watching the first episode with him, with a feeling of horror, as Ganga drowns seven of the sons she has borne to Shantanu, one after the other, having extracted a promise from him that he will not question any of her actions. The explanation in the myth is that she is saving them, and Shantanu, from a curse; but the visual impact of a woman drowning seven babies in succession was nothing short of horrific. The eighth son, who is not killed, is Bhishma, the grand patriarch of the

Mahabharata; he lives to a great age and sees his descendants enter into a destructive internecine war.

At the time we were all preoccupied with the rise of communal tension in the country, and the overt attempt to whip it up by a Hindu nationalist party entering the political arena as a serious player. The *Ramayana* is an epic that many Hindus take to heart, and it has been recounted in several versions: from the perspective of Sita, of Ravana, of Shambuka, who is killed by Rama because he dared to aspire to learning, performing harsh penances in order to gain knowledge. We have the Kamban *Ramayana*, north-eastern *Ramayanas*, Indonesian and Thai *Ramayanas*. There is the sentimental *Geet Ramayan* in Marathi, composed by G D Madgulkar, with a strong Brahmanical ethos, dear to the hearts of middle-class Maharashtrians.

This multiplicity of versions is sometimes cited as proof of Hinduism's pluralism and tolerance; but it is the *Ramayana* of Valmiki, and in north India the *Ramcharitmanas* of Tulsidas, an even more patriarchal rendering, that are the most popular and influential versions. Men do cut off their wives' noses and think that they are acting righteously. The stories that appear alongside the main thread of Rama's exile may, as many scholars have surmised, record historical clashes between ruling regimes and forest-dwellers, and between rival clans. But the story of Shambuka claims an upper-caste monopoly over knowledge. That of Eklavya in the *Mahabharata* teaches the same chilling lesson.

Both the *Ramayana* and *Mahabharata* were composed in layers over long periods of time, with episodes recording some actual historical conflicts and regimes. The claim being made now by Hindutva forces is that the *Ramayana* is a totally historical record and that the site of Rama's birth and reign can be identified today. Of the two epics it is the more unitary story, pivoting around a single hero; but the *Mahabharata* incorporates the *Gita*, which is regarded as the holy book of the Hindus, a book that justifies war, and teaches the art of righteous war that includes lying and deceiving in its cause.

Hinduism and 'son-preference'

The male hero, the Kshatriya warrior, is central to both epics. This is not unusual; most great epics have a male hero. But Hinduism also underlines the importance of a male *heir*; only a son can perform the last rites for a Hindu man or woman. This may not be the only reason for the phenomenon of 'son preference' in modern India; the Hindu marriage is virilocal: the bride moves into the bridegroom's home and becomes a part of his family. Tradition has it that the bride's parents cannot accept hospitality or financial help from their daughter after she is married; it is the son and his wife who will look after them in old age. These traditions, together with the practice of dowry, which has now spread from the upper castes to those lower in the hierarchy, all add up to a strong desire for a son. New technologies have made it possible to identify the sex of a foetus during pregnancy, and over the last twenty years or more, the practice of aborting female foetuses has become so widespread that it has significantly affected the sex ratio of the Indian population.

Violence against women on a daily basis in the form of neglect of the female child in favour of the male; early marriage with early and multiple pregnancies; and a continuous series of deprivations throughout married life, had skewed the sex ratio even before the year 2000. Amartya Sen famously drew attention to this when the 1991 Indian Census showed a ratio of 927 females per 1000 males.[2] But the 2001 Indian Census revealed a new kind of bias: in 1991, the sex ratio for the age group 0 to 6 years had dropped from 945 girls per 1000 boys to 927; in 2011 it was 914. In some districts of Punjab and Haryana, the juvenile sex ratio was below 800 girls to every 1000 boys.[3] By 2020, female foeticide had resulted in a steep fall in the sex ratio in the marriageable age demographic.

One might have thought that this would loosen the rules of caste endogamy or reduce dowry demands; instead, we have seen new kinds of violence emerge as a result of the skewed sex ratio. Girls from less prosperous regions, and sometimes from lower castes, are 'imported' as wives, and treated more or less as domestic servants who perform sexual services for the husband. The prevalent culture of condoning rape and violence against women in general, may also have the low female-male ratio among the young as one of its causes.

Religious, caste and gender-based violence

Rape, disfigurement, blinding, naked parading, burning alive: these are some of the forms of violence that are inflicted on women, and especially women of the lower castes. But, unfortunately, those who man the institutions of the state are also conditioned by the deep-rooted protocols of caste and patriarchy, which are part of the Hindu religious ethic. Caste violence, for example, is only too often condoned through arguments framed in the language of law, but articulating the logic of prejudice.

Bhanwari Devi was a woman employed by the government of Rajasthan in its Women's Development Programme, which trained village women, usually among the poorest or most backward in their communities, to deliver the basic development targets of the government. In 1992, as part of her work, she intervened to prevent a child marriage in an upper-caste family; as a reprisal, she was gang-raped by several men of this caste group. A case was filed in the high court of Jaipur, where defence counsel for the perpetrators argued that men of a higher caste would not be likely to engage in such an act with a woman of low caste, especially when younger men of their families were present.[4]

Following this incident, two major occurrences of anti-Muslim violence, in which state governments were implicated, took place: in Mumbai, from December 1992 to January 1993, after the demolition of Babri Masjid; and in Gujarat in February-March 2002, following the burning of the Sabarmati Express from Godhra to Ahmedabad. The most brutal forms of violence against women took place, with clear evidence of the involvement of the police and other government servants. It needs to be emphasised here, that in both instances, it was *Muslim* women who were deliberately identified and targeted.

In 2006, three persons of the Bhotmange family, Buddhists of the Mahar caste, were murdered by a village mob in Khairlanji, in the district of Bhandara in eastern Maharashtra. The two women, Surekha Bhotmange and her daughter, Priyanka, were gang-raped and their naked bodies left out in the open.

The attack took place on September 29, 2006, but it was not until the beginning of November that the news reached the papers. It was not just the state administration and the courts, the media also colluded in playing down the attack. But because the nature of the violence was horrific, once the news became public there was a spontaneous reaction from Dalit youth all over Maharashtra. Their protest was met with a strict clampdown by the police.[5] Moreover, there were efforts at every level of the government machinery and the courts to destroy evidence and to deny that the crime had any relation to caste. Also, of course, to cast aspersions on the character of the two women. The family was upwardly mobile; Priyanka was doing well at college and rode a bicycle.

What is interesting is that after the month-old news of the Khairlanji massacre exploded, it needed another trigger: the defacement of some statues of Babasaheb Ambedkar in Kanpur, in far-off Uttar Pradesh, before Dalit anger could express itself. This entire sequence of events is a reminder of how much the violence against Dalits (especially sexual violence against Dalit women) has been *normalised*, not just among caste Hindus but in the minds of Dalits themselves. Dalit bodies are cheap; but women's bodies are even cheaper. Dalit suffering is an everyday matter, even when it takes shape in the most brutal form. And yet Dalit anger is a thing to be feared. The Maharashtra state police continued to pick up young Dalit men in cities and towns all through the month of November: those who protested and those marked out as a 'danger to public peace'. The hyped-up fear was that the gathering of thousands of Dalits in Mumbai on December 6, the 50th death anniversary of Dr Ambedkar, would turn violent. A date that could have been marked with grave significance for the nation as a whole, was instead marred by the cover-up of heinous rape and murder and the petty harassment of Dalit protesters.

Shaping perceptions through changing the narrative: this is something the present political regime is very good at. When thousands of Dalits gathered at Bhima-Koregaon on January 1, 2018, to celebrate the 200th anniversary of the defeat of the Peshwas by a British army contingent, in which a number of Mahar soldiers were killed, mainstream media did not focus on how the Mahars had been fighting on the side of the British, or that this was anti-national, and so on. Here the Dalits were putting forward their own narrative, countering the mainstream masculine account of the struggle against the British. Although the Dalit narrative was also masculine, it countered the emasculation of the Dalit male that is one of the lynchpins of caste hierarchy.

The tactic used here was, first, to stir up trouble in the gathering via attacks by some trouble-makers, led, according to many witnesses, by two right-wing (Brahmin) demagogues, Sambhaji Bhide and Milind Ekbote. This provoked some Dalit reaction at the site, and later incidents of stone-throwing, etc., elsewhere. The police arrested many Dalit activists; Dalit leader, Prakash Ambedkar, called for the arrest of Bhide and Ekbote, neither of whom were booked then, or till date. Some months later, the Pune police picked up a number of social activists, allegedly for involvement in the Bhima-Koregaon violence. This is where the change of narrative comes in. The activists, many of them lawyers, had been fighting for the rights of marginalised groups in various places within and outside Maharashtra; on the basis of a pile of questionable evidence they were also accused of working with 'Naxalite' and Maoist groups. Several of them are in jail, others face imminent arrest, their anticipatory bails having been denied.

The actual provocation for the violence at a site where hundreds of thousands of peaceful (but exuberant[6]) demonstrators were gathered has been set aside, while the Dalits who allegedly retaliated are still in jail. The violence of an upper-caste led mob against the caste-marginalised and its cover-up by the state has disappeared completely from public discussion; instead, state and central governments have clamped down on those fighting in the cause of the poor and the marginalised.

However, there is another, painful aspect to the whole sordid affair in my view. Those few persons arrested as 'urban Naxals' are people like us for the liberal public, while the faceless demonstrators who were celebrating an event important in *their* history, are not. Thus, state violence against Dalits has been rendered invisible again—Bhima-Koregaon is no longer about Dalit assertion; it has morphed into being about the detained activists.

Protection, and the covering-up of *communal* violence by the state, on the other hand, is not rendered invisible in the same way. The Muslim is portrayed as the 'enemy', whether as inheritor of the sins of Muslim rulers in the past; as seducers of Hindu girls in the present; as killers of cows and consumers of their flesh; as misguided youth lured by organisations like ISIS; indeed, of scores of other accusations flung around indiscriminately these days. Violence against Muslims is *legitimised*, as long as we can skirt the provisions of the law. State violence against Dalits, on the other hand, cannot be justified in the same way; therefore, it has to be rendered invisible. In this context, at least, liberal carriers of our social conscience seem to play along, by fighting on grounds deliberately and diabolically prepared by the right-wing forces in power.

Hinduism and the psychology of violence

Writing at a time when the party in power subscribes to the aggressive ideology of Hindutva and has consolidated its hold, I have realised two things which I will state here as propositions. First, the recent upsurge of violence against women, Dalits and Muslims, as well as against other minorities and marginalised sections of society, is a surfacing of the potential for violence that has always been present in a society ruled by Brahmanical Hinduism. I use the term 'Brahmanical Hinduism' for that version of Hinduism that is being peddled to us every day. Within the broader community that can be labelled 'Hindu', there are many sub-traditions—traditions of artisanal knowledge, as celebrated by Kancha Ilaiah; matrilineal traditions; the worship of local gods, either assimilated or not into the Hindu pantheon; different marriage customs and rituals; and so on. But that broad horizontal plurality called Hinduism is fundamentally divided by caste, a vertical hierarchy, with Brahmins at the top. The Brahmanical monopoly on knowledge excludes *other castes and all women* from acquiring or wielding knowledge, where knowledge is power. Moreover, it devalues all other forms of knowledge, as well as those who have worked to attain, and possess, that knowledge. The Hinduism that engages with modernity is perceived as Brahmanical Hinduism; the narrative of 'development', especially over the last thirty years, has been one of homogenisation. The violent destruction of the environment; market-led development, and the decline of folk arts, handicrafts and artisanal traditions; the devaluing of non-Brahmanical cultures; have all had its imprimatur. The contempt of the upper-caste Hindu for lower castes and Dalits is manifest in systematic exclusion and daily humiliation. The violent and deliberate targetting of Dalits, Muslims and women that we have seen recently is just a more extreme manifestation of the contradictions that are woven into the basic structure of Brahmanical Hinduism.

My second contention is that our tolerance of violence against Dalits and women, and of violence against Muslims, is based on two different forms of Othering that Hindutva ideology effectively propagates: the Othering of internal inferiors, and of the external enemy.

At the beginning of this chapter I mentioned some mythical stories from the *Ramayana* and *Mahabbharata*, and the influence they have on Hindus even today. The psychoanalyst and social theorist, Sudhir Kakar, explains their influence as follows:

> In an apparent reversal of a Western pattern, traditional myths are less a source of intellectual and aesthetic satisfaction for the mythologist than of emotional recognition for others, more moving for the patient than for the analyst. Myths in India are not part of a bygone era. ...Vibrantly alive, their symbolic power intact, Indian myths constitute a cultural idiom which aids the individual in the construction and integration of his inner world. [7]

To understand the roots of violence in the Indian psyche, it would be necessary to explore the formation of the Hindu 'inner world'. Psychoanalysis has never been very popular in India as a therapeutic practice; neither have Freud's theories been taken seriously by intellectuals examining the Hindu psyche, or the roots of caste and patriarchy. Ashis Nandy is one of the few who has ventured to do so. Commenting on the question of the recent surge in violence against women, he says:

> For the moment I shall only say this: Not only did women have power in traditional India, which was a phenomenon natural to all agricultural societies, this power came from the religious and 'magical' equation or continuity made in such societies between women's reproductivity and the fertility of land.

> ...The traditional fear of a woman and her access to the primal magical powers of women remained just below the surface. The growing presence, self-assertion and self-confidence of women in the modern sector reactivates these fears, and there is a desperate attempt to put the genie back in the box. The violence comes from that fear.[8]

It is perhaps unsurprising that neither feminists nor critics of the caste system have used the insights of psychoanalytic theory to explore the roots of violence in Hindu mythology. Juliet Mitchell's 1974 book, *Feminism and Psychoanalysis*,[9] in which she counters contemporary feminists' hostility to Freud, points out that his contributions to the understanding of personality development are invaluable for feminism. The American psychoanalyst, Alan Roland, has talked about how different child-rearing practices within the extended family in Indian society can 'differently structure the inner world of Indians'.[10] This inner world is deeply influenced by the patriarchal family and the hierarchically structured system of caste.

In the last chapter, I spoke about how caste Hindus find it difficult to recognise their own privilege. The familiarity and easy availability of help in the homes of the upper castes and the middle classes, creates a specific kind of domestic environment in which there are people who occupy 'our' intimate spaces and yet are very different from 'us'.

The women's movement has raised the question of the gender division of household labour in a general way, but in India those from the lower castes are always available to undertake the most unpleasant and menial work in many households. Outside the urban educated upper-caste elite, however, the women of the household are still expected to do most of the household chores themselves, and this is sometimes expressed as a matter of caste pride: 'In our home we have fresh food cooked at every meal, unlike in upper-caste urban houses.'

It is in the domestic space and in the sphere of sexual intimacy that violence begins. Hindu society makes some cultural space for those who are 'aberrant' in relation to prevalent heterosexuality: hijras or eunuchs traditionally perform at weddings and their asking for alms is looked upon as a cultural 'tradition'. But young men known to be gay by their families will still be 'married off' to unsuspecting girls who are obeying their parents' wishes regarding choice of marriage partner; the rules of caste endogamy and marriage at the 'right' age are rigorously followed. Lesbianism occurs in all strata of society, but it cannot be acknowledged; it must be hidden from the men of the household who may react violently if they find out. This is the nuts and bolts of how caste patriarchy functions at the level of the family, in an often multi-generational household. Things may be changing, as even the RSS has accepted homosexuality; the LGBTQ community has become more outspoken and visible; but there is still violence against those who are sexually deviant. The tradition of silence on the subject of sexuality has not really been broken.

The duplicitous moral base of the Hindu family perpetuates violence against women within the home. Once a girl is married, her own parents often turn a blind eye to physical abuse and ill-treatment by her husband and his family. To have her return to her natal home would be an economic strain *and* a social disgrace. The culture of the Hindu majority influences all others, and so we see functional caste divisions among Sikhs, Muslims and Christians, as well; the important difference is that these practices do not have religious sanction among non-Hindus.

Mainstream feminism in India, with its upper-caste origins, sometimes romanticises the situation of Dalit and Adivasi women who work outside the home and are not subjected to the same controls on their mobility or their sexuality, as upper-caste women are. On the other hand, when Dalit women prioritise caste violence over domestic violence, they are reminded that patriarchy exists among Dalits, too, and are accused of being 'soft' towards 'their' men. Adivasi women may not be considered untouchable, but there are many cases of them being beaten, boycotted, and turned out of their villages on suspicion of being 'witches'. The death of a child or even an animal, a drought or a diseased crop: all are attributed to the actions of 'witches'. Injustice and violence against women in a predominantly Hindu society are entangled with all these: caste, patriarchy, class, identity through Othering, and a religious order that is divided at the very base. We make do with the notion of 'intersectionality', acknowledging that any one woman is caught up in many structures of exploitation, subjugation and Othering; but we do not fully understand how these structures impinge on and implicate one another.

I will repeat, then, that the proliferation of incidents of violence that we have seen in recent years cannot be explained as a result of the politics of Hindutva alone. Hindutva builds on the deep roots of violence in a caste-patriarchal Hindu social order. If we are to reverse this trend and work towards a more open-minded and egalitarian society, we must understand and accept this. It is not enough that the marginalised speak out, we must listen to what they are saying, and learn from it. We must recognise that there are demons within ourselves, and learn to confront them.

My own distancing from my identity as a woman born into a Hindu family took place over time, but not in any single act of rebellion in the way I chose to live my life. My father was an atheist and a liberal who did not impose his ideas about whom I should marry. He even (partially) accepted Tulsi as my husband, a man from a working-class background who had given up a good job to become an activist among Adivasis. This may have been easier for him because my elder sister married a Muslim; *that* had not been so easy to accept. I have not personally suffered violence directly, but I have experienced the divisiveness that is so deeply ingrained in our social fabric, and I have seen how it has affected others. I have also seen how a patriarchal extended family is essentially misogynist, and fails to support the woman who is expected to hold the family together in a crisis. I have experienced how patriarchal values shape relationships among women in the family, and realise that a personal embracing of feminist values is not sufficient to counter this. I have also seen the effect of patriarchal expectations on the male psyche, and understood that it is not just women but also men who suffer from the inequitable values we live by.

It is as a woman who has rejected her Hindu identity that I look at the misogyny, the Islamophobia, and the Brahmanical divisiveness that have put down deep roots in India today. Mine is not a Dalit feminist standpoint, for my life has not been that of a Dalit woman. It is that of an upper-caste woman, a feminist, who has tried to learn from being in that upper-caste location; who accepts that leadership for social change will come from elsewhere, from another generation, another caste, another class. And it is as one such that I have written about why I am not a Hindu woman.

References

[1] Sudhir Sonalkar, '*Ramayana*: A Hermeneutic Study', ICSSR *Research Abstracts Quarterly*, January-June 1994.

[2] Amartya Sen, 'Missing Women', *British Medical Journal*, 304, 1992.

[3] Amartya Sen, 'Missing Women Revisited', *British Medical Journal*, December 2003.

[4] For a recent commentary on this case and its repercussions, see V. Geetha, 'Sexual Harassment and Elusive Justice', *Economic & Political Weekly*, Vol. 52, Issue No. 44, 2017.

[5] Anand Teltumbde, *Khairlanji: A Strange and Bitter Crop* (New Delhi: Navayana), 2008. See also Shivangi Gupta, 'The Khairlanji Massacre Still Continues to Haunt the Brahmanical State', https:

//feminisminindia.com/2019/08/05/khairlanji-massacre-haunt-brahmanical-state/

[6] Somnath Waghmare's documentary, *The Battle of Bhima-Koregaon: An Unending Journey*, though made in 2017, a year before the bicentenary, conveys the exuberant mood of Dalits at this event.

[7] Sudhir Kakar, *Culture and Psyche* (New Delhi: Oxford University Press), 1997.

[8] Ashis Nandy, *The Intimate Enemy: Loss and Recovery of Self Under Colonialism* (New Delhi: Oxford University Press), 2009.

[9] Juliet Mitchell, *Feminism and Psychoanalysis* (New York: Pantheon), 1974.

[10] Alan Roland, 'Psychoanalysis Across Civilizations: A Personal Journey', *Journal of the American Academy of Psychoanalysis*, 31: 275–295, 2003.